LOCAL HIS
SOCIE

ABBOTS LANGLEY PROJECT 2000

Tempora mutantur, nos et mutamur in illis
Times change and we change with them

Abbots Langley Local History Society
2001

First published in 2001 in Great Britain by
Abbots Langley Local History Society
136 Abbots Road, Abbots Langley, Hertfordshire WD5 0BL

ISBN 0-9541652-0-9

*The cover illustration shows, by permission, the Ordnance
Survey map of Abbots Langley for 2000.
© Crown Copyright NC/00/558.*

Edited and compiled by Elizabeth Manning; designed and
typeset by Robin Mann, Abbots Langley Local History Society.
Printed by The Russell Press Ltd, Russell House, Bulwell Lane,
Nottingham NG6 0BT

The Abbots Langley Local History Society is indebted to the *Millennium Festival Awards for All* for their grant which made publication of this book possible.

Clive Clark adds the final touches to his book, *Abbots Langley Then 1760–1960*, in June 1997. Sadly, he died the following year. Photo: Eve Durtnall

Foreword

When in 1994 my late husband Clive was helping to launch the now highly successful Abbots Langley Local History Society, he was already looking forward to the Millennium as a historical event. He felt it would be a suitable opportunity for people to record their memories and their impressions of the village at the end of the twentieth century.

During his thirty-five years of research and study of the local history, he worked through thousands of "official" documents – parish records, memorial records, tax returns, legal documents, and so on. But we know little of what the ordinary people, craftsmen, labourers in the fields, the women, thought of the hard and uncomfortable world in which they lived out their often short lives in earlier centuries. The invention of the camera, and almost universal literacy for the last hundred and fifty years, gives us some idea of more recent times.

Clive, true social historian that he was, was constantly reminding us that without recording and noting passing events, there would be no history for future generations to enjoy. At the same time he said that no history is definitive, there is also more waiting to be discovered by those who go and seek.

During the many days and hours we spent walking the streets and fields around Abbots Langley, Clive himself recorded in notes and pictures the changing scene. It is part, he said, of a wonderful series of stories, and he himself was a master story-teller.

So I am very happy that the present Committee of the Abbots Langley Local History Society has continued with Clive's idea and produced "PROJECT 2000", and I dedicate these writings to his memory and to Abbots Langley and all its people.

In the Book of Remembrance on the anniversary of Clive's death, you can read:

He does not die that can bequeath some influence to the land he knows.

Simonne Clark, March 2000

Acknowledgements

Thanks are expressed to:

- The individual authors, identified at the beginning of each article.

- Prue King for the use of her sketches.

- Eve and Ken Durtnall, Reg Nice, Elizabeth Manning, Pat Holmes, Peter Turner, Doreen Cooper and Mike Quinton for the use of their photographs. Each photograph carries an appropriate credit.

- The Ordnance Survey for the use of the Ordnance Survey map of Abbots Langley for 2000. © Crown Copyright NC/00/558.

- The Local History Press (www.local-history.co.uk) for arranging the printing of this book.

Contents

Page

Foreword...5

Introduction...13

A Day in the Life of the...

Teacher	Penny Franklin	18
Teacher	Kate Quinton	23
Retired Villager	Roger Flint	32
Volunteer	Susan Tomson	40
Postman	Duncan Devlin	50
Mother	Anne Simons	61
Retired Teacher	Pauline Wadl	66
Nurse	Anne Flanders	72
Church Administrator	Pam Rastall	79
Engineering Lecturer	Richard Simons	81
Scholar	Simon Stanley	91
Villager	Rosemary Burrows	101
Methodist Minister	Stephen Fulcher	109
Councillor	Paul Goggins	117
Retired Physicist	Mike Quinton	121
Vicar	Brian Andrews	137
Volunteer	Geoffrey Flanders	142
Butcher	Simon East	149
Villager	Maureen Denton	153
Archivist	Audrey Ashby	168
Tutor	Brian Hibberd	172
Retired GP/Horticulturist	Peter Tomson	176
Family Man	Roger Yapp	182
Milkman	David Miller	186

Places in Abbots Langley

Abbots Langley Pubs..15
Road Transport at the Millennium.....................44
Fieldpaths I Walk...58
Train Travel at the Millennium.........................103
Air Travel at the Millennium 119
The Grand Union Canal Now.............................144
Grand Union Canal at the Millennium.............156

Social Interests

A memorable day..25
The Health Service in Abbots Langley..............38
Lifestyle of an Old Age Pensioner in Abbots Langley.............48
Diary of a building extension at 82 Tibbs Hill Road.............55
Village Photographers 70
A busy weekend..99
Some of the local societies I belong to.............114
Abbots Langley appreciated..............................120
Millennium Eve Party 139
Community Nursing in Abbots Langley at the end
    of the 20th century.......................................152
My life in Abbots Langley in 1999....................160
Retiring early? Not in Abbots Langley,
    we might miss something!.............................169
On being retired in Abbots Langley as the
    Millennium approaches.................................179

Historical Anecdotes

Mansion House Farm..20
Christmas Day in the Bakehouse, 1900s.............37
Memories 1946–1999...52
Abbots Langley Belfry 1899–1900........................73
The Pocket Watch...83
Abbots Langley Bowling Club 84

I remember – VE Day Street Party 1945 112
I was an evacuee in Abbots Langley in World War II 126
End of an era?.. 146
Art Club 165
Nicholas Breakspear Week 189

Technical Features

The Millennium Bug 28
Working with computers at home in Abbots Langley 62
Household appliances in 1999 69
Money, Weights and Measures: changes in 100 years 93
Putting the Abbots Langley Local History Society
    Journal together 106
Household repairs in 1999 124
Nature Notes 174

Alphabetical list of contributors

Brian Andrews..137
Audrey Ashby 106, 168
Peter Avery...20
Sue Avery...169
Wendy Beaumont 152
Rosemary Burrows 101
Marion and Arthur Capon....................................120
Clive Clark 126
Doreen Cooper..144
Maureen Denton..153
Duncan Devlin 50
Eve and Ken Durtnall 70
Simon East..149
Anne Flanders 72
Geoffrey Flanders 142
Roger Flint 32
Penny Franklin..18
Stephen Fulcher 109
Paul Goggins 117
Brian Hibberd...172
Pat Holmes 25, 112
Ray Holmes 25, 146
Peter and Diane Howarth 55
Prue King 165
Alan Johnson 189
Jane Lay 114
Robin Mann...62
Elizabeth Manning.. 93, 160
Tony Manning 44, 48, 103, 119, 156
David Miller...186
Jean Nice 69
Reg Nice 15, 58, 124
Sue and Dave Noise 83, 174
Janet Palmer 99

Mike Quinton 121
Kate Quinton.. 23
Pam Rastall.. 79
Joan Sanders 38
Anne Simons.. 61
Richard Simons.. 81
Simon Stanley.. 91
John Sutton.. 73, 84, 179
Susan Tomson 40
Peter Tomson 176
Peter Turner.. 139
Maud Vine 52
Pauline Wadl.. 66
Roger Yapp.. 28, 182

Introduction

Abbots Langley Project 2000 is a collection of memories of Abbots Langley in the 1900s from people living in Abbots Langley as the century draws to a close.

Historians over the centuries have chronicled all of the great world events – wars, great political changes, the comings and goings of kings and queens, major landmarks in technological progress. Yet they have largely had to guess or deduce from fragmented local sources, what life was like and how the world appeared to the ordinary common people of Abbots Langley and thousands of places like it.

Life one hundred years ago was hard, but simpler and more leisurely. The words "jeans", "trainers", "computer" and "aeroplane" could have come from another planet. In describing what we see now, we are therefore also recording the pace of change. In one hundred years' time, they will doubtless smile at what will be considered our imperfect, disorganised way of life.

At the end of the second millennium of the Christian era we can look back and look forward and make incredible comparisons. For instance, in the last 150 years, universal literacy and the availability of the camera has enabled us, the ordinary people, to record what we do and see in our increasingly complex and busy lives. So our late friend Clive Clark thought that the most appropriate way for our Society to celebrate the millennium would be for us to record, through words and pictures, the most complete picture as possible of the village, the surroundings, the people and what they do, in order to give future generations as accurate an insight into our lives as we can. In this way we can place on record some of the things that are unlikely to be included in official documents, but will serve as a major source of local reference in future years.

The present Committee of the Abbots Langley Local History Society has been dedicated to seeing this project through.

So it is with sincere gratitude to all those people who have contributed their personal record of life in Abbots Langley in the 1900s, that this book is presented for future generations in the hope that they will enjoy these reminiscences of a bygone age!

***

ABBOTS LANGLEY LOCAL HISTORY SOCIETY COMMITTEE MEMBERS 1999-2000

Left to right, sitting: Dr Mike Quinton, Chairman; Audrey Ashby, Journal Editor; Robin Mann, Publications; Standing: Eve Durtnall, Membership Secretary; Geoffrey Flanders; Dr Richard Simons; Tony Manning, Treasurer; Elizabeth Manning; Reg Nice, Secretary
Photo: Ken Durtnall

Abbots Langley Public Houses

Reg Nice

Despite the fact that half-a-dozen pubs in the parish of Abbots Langley have closed during the last forty years or so, there are still plenty from which to choose, varying widely in character, facilities and the type of clientele for which they cater.

Over the last ten years or so, because of the drinking and driving laws, people drink more alcohol at home than in pubs, so pubs have adapted to these changing social conditions by offering, mostly, a wide range of food. Indeed, some have almost become restaurants, though because of their small size, in 1999 none of the Abbots Langley pubs come into that category.

Typically, at the time of writing, the price of most beers is around £2 per pint, wines and spirits about the same. In an average pub, a main meal costs around £6, and a substantial sandwich or snack-type meal available at midday, is usually £3 to £4.

In the village centre, the Boys Home, formerly the Rose and Crown, is a real old-fashioned working men's pub little altered from when it was built around 150 years ago. Purely a "watering hole", it does not serve food, and displayed inside is a good

The Boys Home, 1990. Photo: Eve Durtnall

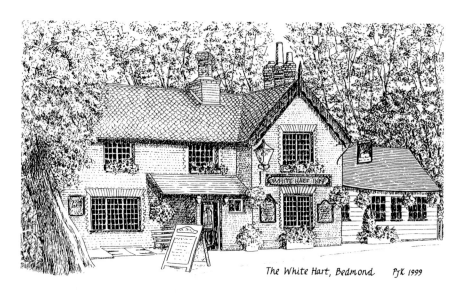

The White Hart, Bedmond   PJK 1999

collection of military artefacts. The licensee is David Allery, an Abbots Langley born and bred man.

Nearby, the rebuilt King's Head, which replaced the original pub pulled down 35 years ago for road widening, has a different character and appearance altogether and caters for a different clientele in an atmosphere enjoyed by much younger generations by providing such entertainment as karaoke evenings and quiz nights.

A short distance away is the Royal Oak, standing back from the road on Kitters Green, of 18th century origins. About ten years ago it was refurbished, and in pleasant and comfortable surroundings the publican serves good value-for-money meals.

Down towards the valley is a pretty and agreeable 18th century pub called the Unicorn, and further on into Hunton Bridge only two pubs remain of the four which once were there: the Victorian Dog and Partridge and the King's Head. This last pub is possibly 17th century, quite large, backing onto the Grand Union Canal, and as it stands on the line of the old Turnpike it was probably a coaching stop before the railway age. The King's Head serves lunches and evening meals to suit all tastes and purses.

In Bedmond village there are two pubs, the Bell and the White Hart. The former is 16th century and is the oldest pub in the parish, while the latter lays claim to being of that era though does not show many signs of it.

A little to the north, in Pimlico hamlet, is the Swan – of no particular architectural merit, it obviously was built originally to serve the farming people of the area. Good beer and food are served there and it has an agreeable and friendly ambience.

Back in Abbots Langley the Compasses pub near Trowley Bottom stands on what is now a very busy road, at a bus stop, and competes for local custom with the Swan, a few minutes away on College Road which also serves lunches and early evening meals.

There remain to be mentioned various clubs where the drinks are often much cheaper, but for members only and with limited opening times. The most popular are the Abbots Langley Men's

The King's Head, Hunton Bridge

Club, in Trowley Rise, and the Cricket Club, on the Manor House ground.

To sum up, pubs and clubs vary a lot, often different at lunchtimes to evenings and weekends, but they are still an important element in community social life.

A day in my life, May 1999

Penny Franklin

I am a wife, mother of two teenagers, and a support and supply teacher, aged 47. My day begins at 6.55 am when the alarm goes off and I switch on the TV for the early morning news – and I immediately nod off! Husband Peter is away in Germany, Hollie (fourteen in four days' time) grabs the shower and so I go downstairs and make tea and start her breakfast boiled egg, and then get washed and dressed. I see Hollie off to school – late again, but then so is her lift. Take a second cup of tea and a croissant for breakfast, and then panic for five minutes when I can't find the car keys, and then off to school at Tanners Wood nearby.

By 8.55 the children are in, and as supply support this week I help in the administration of Key Stage 1 SATs tests. Class teacher Sarah Honey takes a third of the class out at a time for their first Comprehension paper while I spend time with another third looking at a past paper while the rest of the class continue with their SPMG maths work. We rotate groups across the morning and every child has completed the first section of the paper by lunchtime, although we only had time to make coffee and drink it on the run.

Lunchtime at 12 noon sees me busy marking maths work and looking at SATs answers for twenty minutes in the staff room, snatching a quick Tuna Pasta and a fudge yoghurt. By 12.55 it's time for Register, and Group 1 go out for the second part of the

Comprehension paper. I calmed everyone else down with a story –
"Amazing Grace". The afternoon activities rotate every twenty
minutes to cover three or four of the following: "All About Me"
sheet for personal profiles, writing corner, pastel drawings of
plants being grown in class, construction with multi-link cubes,
farm corner, or floor puzzles. Afternoon play, followed by "Show
and Tell" by Exciting group. We congratulate every child for their
hard work today, and Ross has sweets to hand out to celebrate his
birthday.

At 3.15 it's hometime, and I have a quick chat with Sarah and
finish tidying the classroom, drive to Abbots Langley Library to
return a video, and then on to Parmiter's School to collect Hollie
and transport her to the Watford School of Music for her 4.15
piano lesson. I can relax for a few moments in the student room
with "Polly" by Freya North, a can of Pepsi and a currant bun but
then it's time to drive home via Abbots Langley to pick up another
video, "Sliding Doors".

We're home at 5.30 for a cup of tea and can spend thirty
minutes watching a TV programme about tourists in London.
Peter phones from Germany to say his visit has been mostly
successful and he should be home via the Channel Tunnel by
6 pm tomorrow. At 6.15 it's time to start tea, that is pre-prepared
sweet and sour chicken with rice, and I save a portion for son
Jonathan (18) to reheat when he comes in from monitoring at the
new skate park in Croxley Green. Hollie and I eat while watching
"Heartbreak High" on television, and then quickly wash up and
tidy.

This evening at 7.30 nine of Hollie's friends from the Parish
Youth Group (PYGs) arrive for a video evening get together, and I
watch "Eastenders" and only moan twice about the behaviour in
the next room!! Then it's time to watch "Brookside" and have a
cup of coffee and a chocolate. Jonathan comes home, talks to the
boys and heats his tea, and settles to watch alongside the others.
Noise level certainly subsides! I potter around, cleaning up,
sorting washing and putting clean things away and sigh over the
state of Jonathan's room! At 9.15 parents arrive to collect their

offspring and offer thanks, and by 9.30 they have all gone. I can leave Jonathan in charge, with strict instructions to Hollie to be in bed by 10.

I drive down to "Frankie and Benny's" restaurant in Garston to join a friend's birthday meal. Edwidge is 49 tomorrow and not moaning too much. There are ten of us in all, and I arrive in time to order a rich chocolate brownie dessert and coffee. Loads of chat and fun, and we realise at 11.15 that we are the only ones left and all the chairs are up! Hasty goodbyes, drive home and get in at 11.30.

Put out some peanuts for our nightly hedgehog visitors, fill my hot water bottle, put in a wash load and lock up securely. To bed with "Polly" for ten minutes and then it's lights out just before midnight.

Mansion House Farm

Peter H Avery

As the millennium approaches, the name of the Mansion House Farm will continue to appear on maps as it has done for well over 250 years – although it was originally called "Thorns", back in the 18th century. I am informed that the oldest part of the house is the middle section which dates from about 1670. The addition on the south side carries the date 1752 on the chimney breast.

Work to convert the old Queen Anne farmhouse began in 1986, and the house, barn and stable block now comprise six attractive dwellings. There must be some sadness that the links with the past no longer exist. Some of the older residents of the village remember the old pond to the rear where the boy scouts often met, the haystacks which provided hay for bedding for pets, and the large bull, complete with nasal ornament which stood at the end of the stables.

Mansion House Farm, Abbots Langley

We moved into No.3 in the glorious summer of 1989. Before long I was tackling the triffid-like growth around the old dew pond. Nettles, docks and brambles abounded, well over eight feet high. Indeed, annually, brambles continue to sprout up at alarming rates and with great persistence. Could this be the origin of the name "Thorns" perhaps? Many people who visit our garden on open-days are amazed at the changes that have taken place in the old farmyard. However I am constantly reminded of its previous life by the curiosities I unearth while

Mansion House Farm, Abbots Langley   PJK '99

Mansion House Farm, 1995. Photo: Eve Durtnall

digging. A pair of cleaned-up carthorse traces now adorns our lounge wall, and I have turned up many bones and old bottles. The shallow soil in the front garden is a constant reminder that it was the yard where the cows waited to be milked in the dairy – now our kitchen. Elsewhere the soil is superbly rich, and will grow almost anything.

The wildlife, which seemed to disappear during the period of conversion, is again flourishing. We have visits from foxes, badgers, squirrels, and on at least one occasion a muntjak deer. The many frogs and newts in the pond are regularly culled by our resident heron, who as far as I know is yet to have its first taste of grass snake, visible each summer around the pond area. Woodpeckers, jays, wrens, moorhens and wagtails, as well as the more common birds, all nest nearby.

Recently, the adjacent field, with its derelict barn housing all types of old farm machinery, was completely cleared to form a ménage. Smart new stables house at least a dozen fine privately-owned horses, giving much equestrian pleasure to their owners and riders.

There have certainly been changes, but not all for the worse. As the century closes, the rural environment and the creatures which inhabit it are still in evidence. I think this maintains the link with the past and the people who once knew it as a working farm.

A day in the life of a Biology Teacher

Kate Quinton

It's November, and at 6.20 am the alarm shrills – another day! Helped by a cup of tea expertly made by my husband, Mike, I leave the house at 7.15 and make it into the car accompanied by various bags, keys and an umbrella. The clocks moved back an hour at the weekend and it is a lovely sunny morning as I drive along the spine road through Leavesden, reflecting how appropriate that is for a biologist. There is activity at Leavesden Studios and I wonder if they will survive another year – let alone a hundred years. I drive through Watford, past the town hall and on to Northwood. I arrive at St Helen's School and swing into the lab car park and space number 17 – car parking spaces are very precious.

I unlock the side door and go into the science building, checking that the gas supply to the labs is switched on. I make sure that I am organised for the day. I do some photocopying and greet various staff and technicians as they arrive. At about 8.15 am I pick up my hymn book, diary and class folder and walk over to the main buildings where I collect my post from my pigeonhole, sort it and file it, some in my folder and some in the bin. I then read the notice board and talk to other members of staff. At 8.30 a bell rings and I take my register and go along two corridors to my form room. Here I discover that it is one of the girls' eighteenth birthday and she is surrounded by balloons and presents, most of them edible. We sing "Happy Birthday" not very tunefully and then go round to the main hall for assembly. Today we have some Japanese visitors who sing their school song for us, before spending the day with Year 9.

Back at the labs I embark on my first lesson, a practical on food tests with Year 10 (fourteen-year olds). Apart from a few broken test tubes and some slightly peculiar results, it is successful and they write up and evaluate their work. It is then time for break, coffee and a quick chat with other members of the department. I then have a free period which I spend sorting out an A-level experiment on ripening fruit with my lab technician and arranging for her to buy and store twelve pineapples at different temperatures, and to prepare the rest of the apparatus. The next lesson is one on genetics with a Year 11 class; we discuss sickle cell anaemia and malaria, and sex-linked conditions like haemophilia and colour blindness, finishing the session with practice questions. A five-minute break and then the final lesson of the morning, an Upper Sixth class, where I take in their hypotheses and methods for the investigation into proteolytic enzymes in pineapples that they have prepared over half term. I will mark these before they carry out the experiment. We then return to water movement in plants and the cohesion theory, until the bell goes for lunch time.

I sort myself out for the afternoon before going to the main building for lunch, where I take the opportunity to sit with colleagues from other departments – the science block is isolated so it is good to meet other people. During afternoon registration I notice that it is pouring with rain. Staying in the science block might have been a better idea, as I get soaked returning for lessons. First of all it is a support lesson for Year 13, which this week is for potential medical students about to go to interview at university. We discuss sensitive issues like the use of funds in the National Health Service (NHS), the problems of an ageing population, and the MMR (measles, mumps and rubella) vaccine. The last lesson of the day is a Year 12 A-level practical on the Gram staining technique in bacteria using fresh yoghurt – the Waitrose supermarket down the road is extremely useful, although they must wonder how we use some of the strange things we buy. The girls stain the bacteria and we use oil immersion lenses to look at the results. Some of them have good slides, showing that they followed the instructions meticulously.

At four o'clock I leave smartly – the sooner one drives through Watford at that time of day the better. Arriving home I enjoy a cup of tea with my husband (this is where the day started!). We prepare and eat dinner together and then Mike goes to a talk at Kodak in Hemel Hempstead while I settle down to marking school work and lesson preparation.

A Memorable Day

Ray and Pat Holmes

Our choice of occasion needed no discussion on our part, for as grandparents we certainly enjoyed the privilege of attending our grandson's wedding. Glenn and Sarah, his bride-to-be, held very strong ideas about arrangements for their special day. Where possible, forgotten village customs should be revived. Few would be surprised at such thoughts, if they truly knew the couple personally.

So on August 14, 1999 at their quaint village church of St Bartholomews in Wigginton, invited guests and friends gathered to wish Glenn and Sarah well for the future. Reverend Rob Varty proved to be a credit to his profession. Although his tiny picturesque church barely held the congregation of one hundred and twenty, like the minister it lacked nothing.

On this her important day, Sarah chose to take her father's arm to walk through their village, leading the bridesmaids. The bridal party moved from footpath into church, then down the aisle, finally to stand before a friendly minister alongside her happy groom.

Bidding everyone a warm welcome Reverend Varty added a gentle reminder as to our purpose for gathering this day, slipping conveniently into the wedding service.

Busy ushers had earlier distributed imitation parchment scrolls fastened by strips of beige ribbon which when untied made available the Order of Church Service suitably printed to meet the occasion in fancy Old English.

Traditional hymns aroused many an aged vocal chord, especially when sung with gusto. Readings and quotations listed in "Order of Service" came and went

Those awaiting that emotional pause before those two words ... "I do" were surely well satisfied. On that day two voices full of confidence rang clearly throughout that holy building.

Register witnessed and signed, our Newlyweds reappeared from inside the vestry. Camera time had arrived.

Outside, grey flintstone walls – sought after by many photographers for background material – came once again in demand. Yet, for anyone interested, those flint walls displayed a record of structural alterations. For Wigginton's house of prayer had occupied that plot of land for centuries. Standing there quietly viewing one might imagine changing styles of bridal dress down through the ages. Today would be no exception.

Sarah's bouquet of silver tea roses, supported by eucalyptus leaves, blended nicely with our bride's long sleek satin dress in royal champagne. In allowing her bridesmaids to enjoy an identical style of dress in cream champagne, the bride certainly gained their gratitude. More so, knowing that each dress would double-up as an attractive evening gown later.

Also the gentlemen – groom, both fathers, and ushers – all attended in morning suits, each bearing a silver tea rose in their lapel. Apparently everyone had agreed to dispense with "toppers".

Hundreds of photographs were certainly taken that afternoon, until a halt was called as rain stopped play. Car parking thoughtfully arranged for guests on arrival had also encouraged them to walk leisurely into the village and church. Now, a hurried return to the reception marquee was top priority.

Positioned adjacent to our parking area stood an impressive marquee. Undeniably it claimed attention of anyone passing, and those who had made an early arrival could benefit from a preview of reception facilities. Sunshine illuminated interior decoration, while standing neatly arranged outside the porch entrance stood tubs of flowers – red geraniums in contrast with white surfinas, standard fuschias set between candle lanterns dangling from support posts. Only shades of evening would reveal their value.

But now people returning from church briskly hurried by to assemble beneath the reception marquee. Here inside "Congratulation" banners hung up high alongside bottle-shaped balloons filled with helium. Sprigs of natural ivy twisted upwards on the two main stanchions and all around differing types of decoration enlivened the interior, including table decor.

"Please be seated" came a voice through that chattering hubbub. Readily obeyed by guests, it allowed our caterers to serve a delightful meal.

"Wined and dined" we entered that customary period known as Speech Time. When called upon, Glenn quickly captured everyone's imagination as he delved into the humorous experiences Sarah and he had endured as backpackers across Europe – a very entertaining topic, and one that caused a warm response from his listeners. Other friends of the couple followed suit, presenting witty words of appreciation, while contributing to an amusing passage in that evening.

Barn dancing followed, music being provided by a local group and caller, and quickly people were whirling to and fro across a flooring of thick coconut mats. Sounds of gaiety, shrills of laughter filled the air, destined to continue for many hours.

In the big world outside that marquee candle lanterns now displayed their value and beauty with flickering flames, although in the background a busy generator chugged away keeping power flowing to those essentials of life today such as refrigerators, interior and exterior lighting, toilets, etc. All had taken hours to plan and install.

Yet two days on, only a grass field and memories would survive.

But, what a wonderful and memorable day we had shared together.

The Millennium Bug

Roger Yapp

My name is Roger Yapp and I live at 4 Mainspring, Langley Lane, Abbots Langley together with my wife Jonquil. At present my nineteen-year old daughter, Francine, is away living in Israel before she contemplates returning to full time education. I have been a member of the Local History Society since it started in 1994.

I work for the Canada Life Assurance Company in Potters Bar as the Network Services Manager. I am responsible for the maintenance and development of the United Kingdom computer communications network as well as all of the computer equipment at the Potters Bar headquarters and its branches.

This piece, although not specific to Abbots Langley, has relevance as the "Millennium Bug" was a major feature of the progression to the Third Millennium, and could have impacted the life of each and every one of the village's population. As the world prepared to celebrate the new century I have detailed how I was involved in the final preparations to combat "The Bug".

30th December 1999

Throughout 1998 and 1999 my Team has been heavily involved ensuring that Canada Life's computers will continue to operate in the year 2000, and avoid the problems which are expected to be caused by the "Millennium Bug". Many computer programs which have been developed in the 1980s and 1990s include instructions which refer to date information using only the last two digits of the date – for example 1984 is coded as 84. When the actual date moves into the 21st century, many of these programs will be unable to understand if 84 refers to 1984 or 2084, and hence many problems are possible. Together with many organisations throughout the world Canada Life has embarked on a project to check all computer programs and equipment to ensure that they will work correctly in the new Millennium. This has been a massive effort, involving over 150 people at Canada Life, and costing over £10 million and has been known as the "Y2K Project".

So as the world eagerly prepares for the new century, many people who work with computers await the new Millennium with trepidation, hoping that all of their checking and preparation has been completed successfully. As the clock ticks past midnight on 31st December 1999, the clocks in millions of computers will change to 1st January 2000, and from then on their operating systems and applications software may or may not function correctly. This will not only affect office personal computers and mainframes, it will also affect many other aspects of day-to-day life where computers are built into aircraft navigation systems; power station and water company control systems; air conditioning and lift systems, etc., etc. In addition the "Prophets of Doom" have been predicting that there will be a breakdown of civilization with power failures and water shortages. Bank cash machines will fail to dispense money, and computer failures will cause petrol stations to be unable to provide fuel. One thing will lead to another and the police have been put on standby to be ready to deal with civil unrest.

Thursday 30th December is the last normal working day of the 20th century for Canada Life, as New Year's Eve was deemed a Bank Holiday. Most of the staff left the offices (not to return until 4th January) ready to participate in the many and varied festivities planned to commemorate the new Millennium. Meanwhile the Y2K Project Team looked forward to a very different

Millennium. The pressures to meet the deadlines to check, test
and fix everything had been considerable, and to be perfectly frank
the Team are sick and tired of Y2K. In addition the Team are
scheduled to be back in the office at 11.00 on Saturday 1st
January, so they will have to moderate their celebrations on New
Year's Eve.

31st December 1999

Throughout the day as various parts of the world moved into the
new Millennium it became apparent that the predicted disasters
were failing to materialise. The first major countries passing into
2000 were New Zealand and Australia. They moved into 2000 by
13.00 hours Greenwich Meantime, and the eyes of the world were
on them not just to marvel at their spectacular celebrations, but
also to establish the status of the "Millennium Bug". To everyone's
great relief nothing serious was reported, and as more and more of
the world, including countries which had undertaken very limited
testing, entered the Third Millennium, the status remained
unchanged. Planes were not falling out of the sky, power stations
were still producing electricity, and the world concentrated on
celebrating the Great Event. The "Millennium Bug" was becoming
something of a non event.

Despite having to work on Millennium morning Jonquil and I
did not miss out on the celebrations. Along with many people in
Abbots Langley we decided to spend the Millennium with friends,
instead of travelling to London to watch the celebrations first
hand. It was rumoured that over three million people would travel
to London to watch the massive fireworks display and the "River of
Fire", the opening of the giant "London Eye" Ferris wheel by the
side of the River Thames and the Millennium Dome, further
downstream at Greenwich. Getting there, getting around and
getting home would be very difficult, and with rain forecast we
decided that we would stay in Abbots Langley. We also decided
against visiting the local pubs and restaurants who had massively
inflated their prices for New Year's Eve. Some pubs were charging
£60 for entry on Millennium Night, the local Indian restaurants

were providing a Celebration Menu at £75 per head, and night clubs in Watford were originally offering tickets at £250 each for their celebrations. Many people shunned these offers and as New Year's Eve approached the prices began to fall. However by then plans had been made and many people decided to celebrate locally, thus avoiding the need to "drink and drive".

We celebrated the New Year with our neighbours – John and Irene Field – and their family. Unfortunately many of the family had gone down with 'flu over the Christmas period, but nearly everyone made it to John's in time for the midnight fireworks display and champagne. At the stroke of midnight the sky was ablaze with fireworks. I've not seen so many fireworks in the village sky before – maybe this will become an annual event, and not something to be confined to Guy Fawkes Night on 5th November. As the fireworks lit the night sky, so the Canada Life computers' dates all moved into the Year 2000. What would we find when we returned to work the next morning?

1st January 2000

The Y2K Team assembled at the Canada Life offices at 11.00 am. From about 8.00 am the Building Services and Health and Safety Teams had checked that the electrical and water systems were still operational, that the lifts and fire alarm systems were working, and that it was safe for staff to re-occupy the building. The Y2K Team spent the day checking the systems, but failed to find that the "Millennium Bug" had been at work. Everything functioned as it should. At the same time teams were carrying out the same checks at organisations throughout the UK, Europe and also in North America, as by this time that continent had moved into 2000. Few problems were found, and certainly nothing serious appears to have been found anywhere in the world.

So the questions inevitably will be asked – did "The Bug" ever exist? Was it just hype and paranoia?

In my view I'm certain that if we hadn't checked things and made a number of changes we would have had problems – we would have been collecting premiums for policies and been paying out policy-holders on the wrong dates. Throughout the world there was a massive amount of similar work, which prepared the way, and maybe more effects will become obvious as the world returns to work and as the year unfolds. Thankfully though the "Millennium Bug" has proved to be the biggest non-event at the end of the 20th century.

A typical day in my life in 1999

Roger Flint

I get up at around 7 am regardless of whether it is summer or winter. After more than forty years working for Kodak at Harrow and having to leave home early in the morning it is still difficult to break old habits, even after six years of retirement. Breakfast is usually just a bowl of cereal and is eaten in the kitchen listening to Radio 4 and the Today programme. Before I walk to the village to get my Times newspaper I take my wife, Mary, a cup of coffee. She likes to have an extra hour in bed and usually surfaces at around 8.30 am. My routine is to walk to the village up the Abbots Road, and return via the footpaths through St Lawrence churchyard. This gives me the opportunity to look out for wildlife such as grey squirrels, foxes and different species of birds, in particular the green woodpecker and nuthatches that frequent that area. On my return home I quickly scan the newspaper catching up on the latest news both abroad and in this country, followed by a close scrutiny of the sports pages. I usually find time over a cup of coffee to do the Times Two crossword, or at least as much as possible leaving perhaps a few unsolved clues for Mary. I still find it impossible to complete the Times cryptic crossword.

Today perhaps is my gardening morning at the Hospice of St Francis at Berkhamsted. The Hospice was established to provide a high standard of palliative and respite care to enhance the lives of those suffering from cancer and other life-threatening illnesses. I belong to a team of eight volunteers, who under the direction of Joan Gentry (also from Abbots Langley) maintain the extensive gardens at the Hospice. Joan and I usually travel together by car and find the new Kings Langley by-pass has reduced our travelling time by nearly half. The team of predominantly men do whatever is necessary to keep the gardens well maintained and attractive. Grass cutting is a major job and takes two men two hours to complete. We are all retired and feel that this is one way of putting back a little into the community. The care given by the Hospice to its patients and their families is completely free of charge, and therefore they rely on the generous support of the public. It's amazing how just a few hours work each week by a dedicated band of helpers can transform a garden and provide a peaceful and beautiful environment for those who use the Hospice.

On my return home I usually grab a quick sandwich and a drink of coffee before going out to deliver medication and maybe oxygen for Moss's (formerly Tapsters) the local chemist. Again, this is a voluntary job that I have been doing since I retired. It involves collecting medication and/or compressed gas cylinders of oxygen from the chemist and delivering them to those who require them. Major deliveries of medicines are to sheltered homes where residents need constant supervision and regular medication. Many of these folk came from Leavesden Mental Hospital and for a variety of reasons were not released into the community when the hospital was closed down. Other places that I deliver to are nursing homes and sheltered housing for older residents. Oxygen is delivered as and when required to patients identified by their GPs as needing it to assist breathing difficulties. Delivery usually involves changing over full for empty cylinders of compressed gas and checking that the flow of gas is correct and that there are no problems. With new recipients some tuition in the working of the cylinder gas flow gauges and reassurance that they can cope with the new-fangled system is necessary. The pleasure and thanks that I get for delivering oxygen makes it very worthwhile.

The remainder of the afternoon is my own! We are not the sort of couple who must spend all our time together; we both have our separate interests and activities. However, we do try whenever possible to keep Thursdays and Fridays clear of regular commitments. I invariably walk up to the village sometime during the day to see what is going on, to meet friends, colleagues and acquaintances and keep up-to-date with local news and events. Having lived all my sixty-four years in and around the village, both the people and the everyday happenings are very important to me. I feel very much part of the village and its community. Invariably I will call in at the Methodist Church to check some detail or sort out a problem with the property. My family have been involved with the church since its establishment in the 1880s, and I feel very privileged to be an active member of the church and to serve on the Finance and Property Committee. The Methodist Church in Abbots Langley works well with the other denominations and plays a significant role in the life of the village and its people.

Frequently in my spare time I will walk the local footpaths. I always have my camera on my shoulder in case something unusual catches my eye. A favourite walk involes crossing the M25 motorway from the Abbots Road, across what we term the Ovaltine fields, down Sheppey Lane (as children we knew it as Policeman's Lane) and down nearly as far as the railway line and then return, crossing back over the M25, past Round Wood (known to locals as Bluebell Wood) and back to the Abbots Road. During the walk I am on the constant look out for pieces of Hertfordshire Pudding Stone to add to my collection at home. These agglomerates were formed as the result of tremendous pressure in the earth's formation and were deposited in this area during glacial movement in the last Ice Age. The forty-five minute stroll brings back vivid memories of the days of my youth when Long Wood hadn't been virtually obliterated by the motorway, and badgers and foxes were numerous, and the gamekeeper's cottage was tucked just into the wood. Steam trains puffed their way to and from Euston Station, and collecting train numbers was a treasured hobby for many boys and girls. There were also thousands of hens roaming free-range over the hillside, and just the remnants of the old hen houses now remain to remind me of those former halcyon days.

Hertfordshire Pudding Stone on display outside the Library, 1989
Photos: Eve Durtnall

HERTFORDSHIRE PUDDING STONE
EXCAVATED DURING CONSTRUCTION OF
ABBOTS LANGLEY SECTION OF
M25 MOTORWAY 1986

Dinner is usually at around 5.30 pm. I am the cook, and Mary does the washing up! I enjoy food, full stop. Therefore preparation and planning of what to eat is never a problem. We are not vegetarians but tend to keep to white meat and fish, however Mary complains that I do not prepare enough vegetables, in particular, greens. I have to admit I have never enjoyed cabbage and brussels sprouts – perhaps a hang-up from school dinners or the wartime, who knows? The occasional glass of wine is enjoyed when friends or family join us for a meal, otherwise we do not partake of alcohol. No doubt this has got a lot to do with our strong Methodist heritage. After our evening meal and watching the BBC1 News we both cat-nap for ten or more minutes. I remember my parents doing this and being horrified. I wonder what my children think of us?

Tonight I go to St Alban's Abbey (Cathedral) for a rehearsal with the St Albans Bach Choir. We both love singing and regard it as a great privilege to rehearse and perform in the Cathedral with the highest calibre soloists and orchestras. In keeping with tradition since its inception in 1924 the choir has the Cathedral's Master of Music as its Honorary Conductor. We travel by car, either in ours or in Sue Tomson's, who lives in The Abbot's House and who is also a choir member. We park at the foot of Holywell Hill and walk up to the Cathedral as parking restrictions now apply to the hill itself. The thrill of joining with nearly two hundred other choir members and producing a fantastic sound that fills the building to the rafters has to be experienced to be believed. If the piece we are performing is accompanied by the Cathedral organ then that really is the icing on the cake. After two hours of concentrated rehearsal we return home at around 10 pm totally shattered, with music coursing through our whole being and ready for a well-earned cup of Ovaltine.

It's not late when I go to bed, and I fall asleep easily but rarely sleep all night long. I am always in bed before Mary, who always needs time to wind down.

Christmas Day in the Bakehouse

*Describing the village bakery at the beginning
of the 20th century*

Notes from an article by Ben Bailey about the Creasy Bakery

Once upon a time, before the days of gas and electric cookers, Christmas was incomplete without a trip to the bakehouse. "Bakehouse cooking" was sometimes advertised in local newspapers by the proprietors of the public steam bakery. The steam was forced along countless pipes, by a central boiler. Members of the public could bring their joints, pies, puddings and cakes for baking for about a penny an item.

Bread baking was done early on Christmas Day in the early 1900s, and so from around 10 am local bakers could provide an essential service. A steady stream of people of all ages would head for their chosen bakers, bearing with them their so precious Christmas fare for cooking. Many would drop off these goodies on their way to church or chapel, and collect them, succulent and cooked to a turn, on their return. A century ago a large turkey cost about ten shillings (50p), a goose cost six shillings (30p) and chickens about three shillings (15p) each; but wages were low and bakehouse cooking – more reliable than the old kitchen ranges – ensured that the outlay on Christmas fare was not endangered.

Most of the homemade cakes which often joined the puddings in the steam bakery would include the silver charms so loved for fortune telling. Whoever found the silver or gold coin was promised a wealthy year ahead; the ring was a sign of a forthcoming marriage for its finder; the key meant a new home, or a new knowledge, the button foretold domestic happiness and the wishbone granted its finder a wish.

It must be admitted that not all these homemade efforts were as tasty as the bakers' own wares. Some puddings were badly made and no art could make them a success. But the baker knew most of his customers well and tried to place each item in the best place to give good results.

Usually the mass Christmas "bake-up" went like clockwork (it was rare for anyone to walk off with the wrong turkey), people enjoying a chat while waiting, others having a quick pint. In icy weather, alas, falls with the precious Christmas fare could prove disastrous. But the kindly baker would have a free cake for good customers as consolation.

The Health Service in Abbots Langley

Joan Sanders

Over forty years ago I first experienced Abbots Langley's National Health Service.

We registered with one set of doctors who worked in the Abbot's House, it sounded like a good address for the village. There was also a second team of doctors working from one of the buildings in the High Street shopping area, who also ran a surgery at School Mead.

How does one choose a doctor? Toss a coin? Ask a neighbour? All the folks in our road were as ignorant as we were, we'd all just moved into newly built houses. Over the years I have found our choice to be a very good one, but I am sure those who chose differently were just as happy.

Eventually the two teams got together and between them bought a house – called Vine House, since there had been a large vine growing on the back wall. A flat-roofed extension was added to provide a waiting room and people could now make appointments. A nurse-receptionist was employed, and surgery was held between 9 am and 10.30 am, and 5 am and 6.30 pm. Of course, the

Doctors' Surgery and Health Centre, High Street, February 2000. Photo: Reg Nice

sessions didn't end on time. People's needs vary and doctors often worked on till 11 or 12 in the morning, and house calls were made in the afternoon unless really urgent.

Then, I was asked if I'd like to join the team, as 2nd practice nurse. The work was building up. I had worked in my training hospital for eight years, and my second child was now just five years old and off to school.

Friends of mine thought the work would be boring, but I found there was so much variety from checking pregnant mums to comforting bereaved relatives, immunising babies and assisting with minor surgery. We acquired new equipment and diagnostic apparatus over the years, an ECG machine, a defibrillator.

The senior partners took on trainees (fully trained doctors who wanted to become general practitioners) and the team became larger as district nurses and health visitors took up residence in the surgery premises. So, the house next door was added to the site and a corridor was constructed to join the two buildings. We kept up with modern trends by buying a computer – now extended to provide screens in every room. Doctors can now press a button or two to glean information on past history.

I, and all the original doctors and staff, have now retired, but the modern team has forged ahead, having the whole building revamped, and extending surgery hours considerably.

One hears about wonderful service, and also about unsatisfactory treatment, of course – but it was ever thus. Never will everyone be happy all the time. I feel that the NHS has always been an excellent organisation and would be very sad if it was wrecked by political manoeuvres.

The old vine may no longer exist, but the branching vine of medical services grows wider every day. I hope it serves us well.

A day in my life,
10th December 1999

Susan Tomson

After breakfast, which for me consists of muesli and a slice of toast and a pot of Earl Grey tea, I attempted to finish reading the papers – always hard work on Fridays as there are three of them. I glanced through the Watford Observer, read most of the Independent, and left the Church Times for lunchtime. Then the post arrived; apart from some Christmas cards, there was a letter from the Hardy Plant Society which required immediate attention: a form to be completed describing our garden, which will be circulated to other members in the Gardens Open to the Public leaflet, and another form about offering bed and breakfast to Hardy Plant Society members. Both forms were to be returned by 11 December!

Peter and I discussed how wide an extension to a flower bed

Susan and Peter Tomson in their Abbot's House garden, 1999. Photo: Reg Nice

should be and unfortunately there is a large concrete block six inches underground; do we attempt to remove it? Or just plant shallow rooting plants there? Decisions, decisions.

I drove to Watford having loaded the car with surplus curtains and various books no longer needed by us to deliver to the Oxfam shop, and stopped on the way to drop off a Christmas bottle to my hairdresser, Andy, who was very grateful. On the way I listened to a tape recently given to us by a Godson, called "In your Garden" by Vita Sackville-West. The tape is made up of articles which were printed in the Observer newspaper in the 1940s and 1950s, and makes fascinating listening. Many of the plants are grown in our garden – the main differences seemed to be the price of bulbs and seeds, and of course the prices were given in the old currency – pounds, shillings and pence. For instance, sixpence for a packet of seeds (2p) ranging to two shillings and sixpence (12p) which would have been regarded as very expensive.

Having off-loaded my donated items to Oxfam I parked my car in Sainsbury's and walked down to the Bank to pay in some rent money from two tenants. In Books Books Books I found several Christmas presents – this is a 'remainders' shop, new books at knock-down prices (£2, £3, £4), and I bought two books for one of my daughters-in-law on portrait painting and several books for the grandchildren and great nieces, and also for Josiah who will be spending New Year with us.

The market was busy, as ever, but the bustle and chatter is all part of the fun and my favourite stalls, namely the fish stall and fruit stall, were not too busy. Fish is expensive at present due to the rough weather, but I bought enough for a fish pie and for Friday's supper. The fruit stall is excellent, and as Peter eats bananas as if there is no tomorrow, I stock up for the week at the market – prices there are much better than in Abbots Langley village. Three pounds of bananas cost £1.00 in the market, and in the village are at least 65p per pound.

I arrived back at the Oxfam shop with a little time to spare, which was as well as having eaten my sandwich I was ready to go into the shop at 1.15 pm. Eve, my co-worker for the last four years, has recently had a major operation, and I fear that she won't be back for ages, if at all. So I was 'on' with Pat, the Manager, and for part of the afternoon with Laurence who is French; he is mighty efficient, but not very outgoing. However, there was plenty to do and the takings for the day were over £1500 which was good. Although the shop sells a lot of trading goods, there were many books sold and also quite a lot of clothes – both men's and women's. And, of course, a great many Christmas cards and wrapping paper, as one might expect.

Luckily the Manager did the cashing up, and we were ready to leave the shop by 5.25 pm at which time I did a mad rush in Sainsbury's to buy a few extra goods. Home at last, and having unloaded the shopping I thought about cooking supper. Mercifully we were not going out so as it was Friday night I had a gin and french, which is an excellent tipple but which usually sends me to sleep. Tonight was no exception and I even missed the gardening programme and only woke up to see who the winner was for the Best Gardener of the Year in Wales.

I did manage to write a few Christmas cards but then decided to nurse my cold, which I had caught from Peter, and went to bed at 11.15 pm.

One of our recent joys has been the redecoration of a bedroom which had previously been decorated by one of our sons when he was about sixteen – he is now nearly thirty-nine! It had had a dark brown ceiling and walls, and 1960s' curtains, brown with patterns of red and yellow on them. By rearranging the furniture and repainting the room – this time a subtle shade called "Sudbury Gold" – and with lighter curtains of a lovely coral colour, the whole room looks different. Although The Abbot's House looks vast from the outside, it is quite compact inside. We have an upstairs sitting room which has a wood-burning stove in it and as the room faces south it is always warm. This is the room with my desk (always overflowing with letters and "things to be done"), Peter's computer, the music centre, the TV and video, and the most comfortable Chesterfield that was often used as a bed by the children's friends! Downstairs we have a lovely formal drawing room (painted a warm red) and dining room (painted a rich blue) – colour is very important to us and luckily the rooms are large enough to take strong colours. But it is the kitchen which remains the hub of the house, as it always was when our five children were all at home. The AGA keeps the room warm and the conservatory leading out of it means that there are always plants, colour and quite often scent nearby. We are incredibly lucky to live where we do, and we do rejoice in our good fortune.

Local Transport 1:
Road transport at the Millennium

Tony Manning

Bus outside Henderson Hall, February 2000. Photo: Reg Nice

Dominance of Road Transport

Currently road transport accounts for over 90% of freight movement in the UK and the private car for more than 70% of passenger journeys. The county of Hertfordshire has always held a key position for all forms of transport, lying as it does between London and the other regions of the country. The inhabitants of Abbots Langley have accepted the car as their main means of transport for many years now. Parking is not a serious problem compared to larger conurbations, most dwellings having space for one or more vehicles to be parked off the road, and the area is well served by the national motorway and trunk road system. Two of the principal national roads, the M1 main North South motorway from London and the London Orbital Motorway, M25, which links to the other principal routes leaving London, intersect just outside the parish boundary. As a result typical driving times, outside peak travel rush hours and excluding the time for the necessary refuelling and comfort stops are:-

Dover and Channel Ports	1.5 hours
Brighton	1.5 hours
Coventry	2 hours
Southampton	2 hours
Birmingham	2.5 hours
Bristol	2.5 hours
Cardiff	3 hours
Manchester	3.5 hours
Leeds	3.5 hours
Plymouth	4 hours
Newcastle	4.5 hours
Glasgow	6 hours

Effect on local lifestyle

In the last few years many companies have "out-sourced" some of their requirements. Preparing the annual accounts has long been done by outside accountants for most small and medium enterprises. Now many, including larger organisations, will use specialists for purchasing, advertising and marketing, product design and independent process quality auditing. The specialists may be a partnership or a self-employed individual. Because of its prime position on the national road system, Abbots Langley makes an excellent home base for individuals performing this type of function, as they can readily visit clients by road and spend quite a few hours on site in a single day. Another emerging pattern is for office workers to spend more time working from home, accessing the employing company's operating data via their home computer to do their work, visiting the office for "core time" meetings only. This reduces the need for stressful commuting. Finally, with many

M25 road viaduct over the Gade Valley, February 2000. Photo: Reg Nice

workers changing their employment several times in their working life, settling the family home in Abbots Langley means that it is not likely to be necessary to move house when changing jobs.

Opposition to Road Transport

There is a growing opposition to the continuing growth of road transport, and pressure from various sources, including the government, to switch freight from road to rail or water, and passengers from cars to buses and trains. The opposition is based on the pollution caused by the road vehicles. Giant strides have been made in technology already, with a modern car emitting about 0.5% of the noxious and carcinogenic bi-products of fossil fuel combustion that a car designed thirty years ago would have produced, but it still produces carbon dioxide. The second objection is to the sheer volume of vehicles clogging the streets. It is not a severe problem in Abbots Langley, and the neighbouring towns of Watford, St Albans and Hemel Hempstead can cope, but the city conurbations have a major problem which is being tackled by the reduction of parking spaces and increases in road pricing to force people to use public transport. This problem will not be resolved by the development of the pollution free car. Former car drivers are also reluctant to take to buses which will be subjected to exactly the same frustrating rush hour traffic jams as their car, while costing about twice as much in fares as the marginal cost of using their car for the journey.

The future

Most of us expect to go on using our cars, especially in a semi-rural area like Abbots Langley, although some city dwellers may decide not to run a vehicle, but to hire when they journey outside the city. Goods will still need to be delivered by van. In fact Internet trading is likely to lead to a huge increase in individual van deliveries to homes instead of in bulk to shops, while the shops will expand their home delivery business.

The M25 motorway at a standstill, 1989. Photo: Eve Durtnall

As far as the roads that the vehicles run on are concerned it is unlikely that many entirely new ones will be built, especially in the crowded south east, but existing trunk roads such as the A41 are likely to be expanded to dual carriageway standard throughout their length, while extra lanes will be added to the busiest motorways like the M1 and M25 to ease congestion as traffic grows.

The local bus company has just introduced buses running on gas on some local routes, which represents a cost saving due to the lower excise duty, and means less carbon dioxide is produced with a higher proportion of harmless water vapour to compensate.

Except for individuals working in Central London most residents of Abbots Langley are likely to go on using their cars as their preferred means of transport for the journey to their place of work, for shopping in the village, in the neighbouring towns or the out-of-town shopping centres, and for visits to friends and places of entertainment.

The Lifestyle of an Old Age Pensioner in Abbots Langley in 1999

Tony Manning

I was born in north east London in 1931, educated at the local Technical High School and further educated at the local college, where I met my wife, Elizabeth. After we were married, in common with most of our friends, we moved from the area of our childhood, due mainly to the fact that Town Planning dictated that the London conurbation should not expand beyond its existing boundaries, so that new housing was not generally available.

My first job, in electronic circuit design, was based at Stanmore, so after an initial two years of life in a caravan we opted for a semi-detached house in Abbots Langley, subsequently moving as the family grew, to a larger house nearby. My next job, with a large electronics group, lasted thirteen years and enabled me to build up a pension fund under the company's contributory scheme. Further pension rights were acquired with subsequent employers and also under the State Earnings Related Pension Scheme. As a result I was able to take voluntary retirement at the age of sixty and continued to work part time until, aged sixty five, I retired fully. My wife, like many of her friends, resumed her own career after the family grew up and earned her own pension rights, also retiring at sixty. Our savings were further boosted by the fact that both sets of parents were owner-occupiers, probably the first generation where this was common, and we were able to share in the proceeds of the sale of their homes.

Retirement found us very fortunate in enjoying excellent health and strength and with family finances which would enable us to enjoy an active lifestyle. We are able to continue to live in our current home, which has space to accommodate our children's families when they visit, since like us they have moved away after marriage, and which we can maintain and enjoy, particularly the garden of approximately one-third of an acre which had largely defeated us during our working lives.

Hobbies and activities include golf and tennis for me and handicrafts and family history research for my wife. We are able to attend courses, including residential ones on these hobbies plus, for example, Information Technology to keep up with today's lifestyle. We also enjoy several holidays a year, including foreign travel on a worldwide basis. In the last two years we have been to North and South America, the Middle East, North Africa and many European destinations. Mostly we fly there but we have had motoring holidays, and we have also used the "Eurostar" trains to Europe. Friends in Abbots Langley of a similar age and situation have travelled to South Africa, India, Goa, Australia, New Zealand and Japan, and we also have these destinations as an ambition. Our thirty-year old canal boat is used by us and all members of our family on weekends and for longer cruises up and down the country, every year.

Life is not just one long holiday however, as we are involved in serving a number of societies and organisations in various capacities on a voluntary basis. This again is typical for our generation, and several of our acquaintances also serve as elected representatives in local government. We find ourselves numbered among what is probably the first generation in the history of this country where many ordinary men and women have reached the end of their working lives and raised a family, and now find themselves in good health with an extended life expectancy and a financial situation which provides a reasonable disposable income for the full enjoyment of the time available.

The Working Day of an Abbots Langley Postman, May 1999

Duncan Devlin

My working day begins at 4.15 am when I leave home on my bike to travel to Kings Langley to the Sorting Office to sort the mail for the day.

I arrive at the office at 4.30 am with my colleagues and I firstly sort the mail that I will be delivering, once I have done that any other mail that arrives has to be sorted, and when that is completed I load my bags ready for delivery.

When it is time to leave, my bike is put in the post van, the driver then drops me off at my first delivery point. My delivery consists of 346 delivery points, and with this amount of deliveries I pray for a dry day every day. I get to meet a lot of different people, some going off to work, some walking their dogs. People soon get to know you, as I progress on my round even the school children know me and I often hear the sounds of Postman Pat being called to me.

When the first delivery is finished and I have enough time left, I pop home for a cup of tea. The post van then comes to pick me up

Postman Duncan Devlin on his delivery round, 2000. Photo:
Elizabeth Manning

and take me back to collect the mail for the second delivery and it's the same routine again but on a lighter scale. When the second delivery is finished I am able to go home for my lunch and have a read of the morning paper.

I call in on my mother-in-law to see if she needs any shopping from the village, and I then try and have a rest in the afternoon.

After that I sometimes do a bit of gardening, watch some TV in the evening. There isn't a lot of time to socialise as I have to get up so early in the morning when it all starts again.

Maud B Vine's Memories: 1946–1999

I first came to Abbots Langley after my marriage in January 1946 and settled in Breakspear Road where my husband had a general shop.

I was no stranger to the shop or to Abbots Langley because I had visited quite frequently during the previous two years. However I soon found that visiting a place is quite completely different to living there.

I had arrived from a London hospital where I had completed my training as an SRN (State Registered Nurse) and at the time of resigning was night sister, and so I came to inhabit a completely different world. One thing that surprised me was that everyone knew everyone else whereas in my home town of Wimbledon we hardly knew our neighbours!

It was an extremely cold winter when I arrived and no sooner had I settled in, than my mother-in-law became ill and came to live with us so that I could nurse her. Now she, being a farmer's widow, kept chickens, and as we had a large orchard behind the shop and double garage, the chickens came too! It of course soon became clear who was going to look after them, as well as my mother-in-law!

This was a culture shock, as I lacked any experience in this field and I remember to this day how bitterly cold it was feeding them, breaking the ice on their water twice a day, and how terrified I was of the cockerels! The neighbours and customers must have thought what an odd little "townie" I was!

Anyway my patient's condition soon required a doctor and I learned that a new doctor had arrived in Abbots Road and I went to the Post Office to seek out details; in 1946 very few residents had telephones (we acquired one in 1948 when our first baby was expected) and Brenda Hill (then a young school-leaver, and now is Mrs Whiting and still living in Abbots Road) gave me the information, and so the new doctor arrived at our home.

This doctor was Doctor Haydon senior, and he was full of grumbles about the little village and terrible weather. He was most surprised when I agreed with him, and he soon discovered I too had just arrived from London (the same day as him) and that I was a trained nurse, and so we quickly became friends. So from that time, Dr Haydon would call on my services to care for the "backs" and "heels" of his elderly sick patients, and on occasion would get me to "lay-out" someone who had just died and had lived alone, to make them presentable before the relatives arrived! He introduced me to his son, Eric, who at that time was training at Guy's Medical School, and he of course eventually joined his father in his practice, which was then still in Abbots Road.

In this way I soon got to know many people and I recall how amazed my parents were when they visited and we would go for a walk together, and everyone would speak to me. This, of course, is the difference between living in a town as opposed to a village where the community is so much smaller, and of course we did have a shop and so I quickly got to know the customers and their families. I had also joined the congregation at St Lawrence Church and so my circle of friends and acquaintances expanded rapidly and I really felt part of the village.

In that respect Abbots Langley has never changed; from arriving here in 1946 and still being resident here in 1999 Abbots Langley still remains the most friendly of villages in which to live, and a newcomer is quickly made welcome to the community.

In my first year here I did look forward to visits to my parents' home and I thought Surrey was the best county in England, but it wasn't long before these thoughts changed and I would really long to return to Hertfordshire.

Some things did amaze me when I first came to the village. It wasn't just that everyone knew everyone else, but it was the personal and private things the customers would discuss with my husband and with each other: even matters pertaining to their sex-lives and these conversations would continue outside the shop and in very loud voices! The explanation was of course that at that time most of the villagers had grown up together, been to school together, and in many cases had worked together either at the paper mills or Leavesden Hospital, which was referred to as "working inside"!

Of course all this changed after the Second World War when the council estates were built and there was a greater movement in the population, but I maintain the "friendship and welcome" are still here.

Thinking about life in general in Abbots Langley almost fifty-four years ago, it is strange to remember there were only two residents in Breakspear Road that owned cars. One was Mr Charlie Higgs (father of Brian) and the other was Miss Lottie Buckoke, the schoolteacher; each had an Austin car. Compare that to Breakspear Road today when instead of bicycles propped outside houses, cars line either side of the road from top to bottom!

We as a family grocer made deliveries daily by bicycle, and I can well remember "flying" down through the "poppyfields" – now the Hillside Estate – to deliver in Hunton Bridge.

The changes over fifty-four years are incredible!

Diary of a Building Extension at 82 Tibbs Hill Road

Peter and Diane Howarth

In early 1999 Peter and Diane made the decision to stay in Abbots Langley rather than move back to Norfolk from whence they had come fifteen years previously. But should they move within the village, or stay and improve their "temporary" accommodation that they had lived in for the whole of their time in Abbots? The decision was made to improve their existing house by having a shower room with downstairs lavatory and washing facilities.

Here is the history of that building extension, to show just how long it took from the decision to stay in February 1999, to the – almost – completion of the work on 17 January 2000.

February	House valued £150K. Spoke to builder who advised using an architect. Decided to improve existing house.
March	Architect measured up. Went to Three Rivers Council to get 1/1250 plans.
April	Took 1/1250 plans to architect who was back from hols. Draft plans from architect, which we approved. Finished plans arrived – architect applied for planning permission.
May	Rang three builders for quotations.
June	Local authority inspector came to look at site.
July	Rang two more builders. John Field from Barnesfield Construction came to quote. Quote received from Barnesfield (£12k + VAT). Planning permission received.
August	Accepted Barnesfield quote. (Planned starting date: late October.)

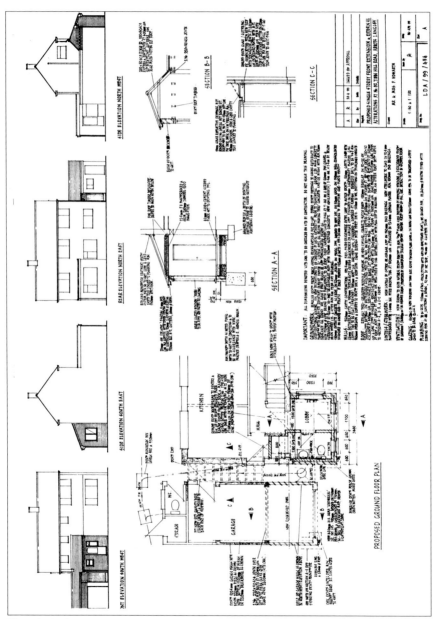

Plans for building extension at 82 Tibbs Hill Road, 26 April 1999

October   Hole in the drive and equipment in the garage. Hole inspected by building inspector. Footings were dug. Footings inspected and concreted. First course of bricks. Old porch being demolished. Unable to locate stop-cock for water supply. Porch completely gone. Chose front door and windows. Skip arrived.

November   Three Valleys Water inspector couldn't find stop-cock either. Roof trusses in place. House and garage now joined by brickwork. Gable end on next-door neighbour's boundary built. Roof tiles arrived and were put up in place. New stop-cock installed. Windows installed. Passage roofed. New down pipes for upstairs bath. Front door fitted. New roof on garage. Knocked through pantry. RSJ (rolled steel joist) installed where old front door used to be.

December   Internal walls built in extension. Electrician installed wiring. Plastered. Shower tray fitted. Plastering finished. Floor screeded. Toilet and wash basin fitted. All working – except shower (still no door to the shower room).

No further work was carried out until after the Christmas and New Year holiday. Work was eventually finished on 17 January 2000, leaving Peter and Diane to decorate and install heating. All the work was carried out by five men with never more than three on site at any one time.

Fieldpaths I Walk

Reg Nice

There are about twenty-two miles (36 km) of public footpaths within the parish. They are mostly maintained by the Abbots Langley Parish Council's workforce, though some are the responsibility of the Hertfordshire County Council.

The paths around the built-up area of the village are nearly all paved, and are very useful short cuts to the village centre from the residential roads. They quite clearly follow the routes of ancient paths used by people going to church or the village from outlying farms and hamlets.

All of the paths are well signposted, and in the fields "waymarked" by coloured arrows on posts provided by the parish council and County Countryside Management Service. They are in good condition, though quickly become muddy in times like the very wet winter of 1998-99 we have just had. They are very well used, not only by local people, but by groups of walkers from elsewhere, following routes published in many guidebooks – such is the popularity of country walking – so there is no fear of the paths falling out of use. Conservation organisations like the Ramblers Association and the Chiltern Society act as watchdogs in matters of access and maintenance.

Because of the size of the parish, it is possible to walk quite long distances using the paths and still staying within the boundaries. My favourite times for walking are in May, when the new growth of spring is everywhere apparent, and the birds in the hedges at their most vociferous; then in August, when there are blackberries in great profusion to be found, and in November when the days are calm and quiet. Clear cold days in January and February can be good also for walking the fieldpaths, when the bare trees can open up dramatic views.

A walk I do frequently starts along the ancient lane to the north of the Abbots Road houses, across Bedmond Road, along Love

Footpath, Abbots Langley to Bedmond, 1998. Photo: Elizabeth Manning

Remaining vestige of Long Wood, looking North, February 2000. Photo: Reg Nice

Lane, across East Lane, now closed to through traffic, then continuing on and crossing the M25; one passes Tenements and Ninnings farms, and then walks on to Bedmond, or alternatively takes the path via Serge Hill and through the pleasant woods back into Bedmond.

Another long walk from the village centre goes northwards across Abbots Road, over the M25 motorway and across Toms Lane and then Hyde Lane, to come near to the telecommunications mast which is visible for miles around. It is then possible to walk past Hyde Farm, and join the western end of Highwood Hall Lane, an old farm road which is now a bridle path – and very muddy and churned up! The reward for negotiating this is the welcome sight of the Swan public house at Pimlico, where good food and beer is available.

In the west of the parish the farm road off Langleybury Lane, opposite the drive to Langleybury Mansion (which until recently was part of Langleybury School) soon becomes a track and is very pleasant indeed. One eventually gets to Bucks Hill, or by turning right and skirting a wood, back into Kings Langley. From Hunton Bridge walking north along the canal towpath is always very interesting with plenty of wildlife and the boats in summer.

The track from behind Abbots Road down to Kings Langley Station is unfortunately very near the M25 with its constant traffic noise, but the view across the Gade valley is superb as we look at land which has been farmed and which has sustained local people for many generations past.

One Day in the Life of a Working Mother and Daughter

Anne Simons

I have lived in the village of Abbots Langley since my marriage nearly seven years ago. I live with my husband and my 4¾-year old son in one of the "old" cottages opposite St Lawrence church. Our house has been occupied by generations of my husband's family who had kept the shop on the property as butchers since the eighteenth century. We are also visited regularly by my sixteen-year old step-daughter who lives in Devon. I work in London four days a week, and on my "day off" – Friday – I visit my elderly father. Here is a typical day "off".

I get up and dressed at 7.45, and wake and dress my son, and then prepare breakfast for the family. At 8.10 I drop my husband off at Kings Langley Station, and drive my son to school outside Hemel Hempstead via the A41, returning home at 9.10 and put the washing on. A quick trip into the garden to add household compost to the compost bin and turn it. Back to the kitchen to complete the washing up and then a telephone call to a friend who has just finished treatment for cancer.

At 11 am I visit my father who lives in a residential home in Rickmansworth. I return home for lunch, clear the fire and get in the coal, sort the washing and at 3 pm leave to collect our son from school. By 6 pm it is time to collect husband from the station, and then prepare supper which we eat together around 7 pm. Then I clear away supper things, and start putting son to bed – finishing around an hour later at 9.30. By 10 o'clock I can watch television for a while, but by 10.30 I am ready to go to bed.

Working with computers at home in Abbots Langley, January 2000

Robin Mann

I work mainly from home and my wife, Hilary, a primary schoolteacher, works part-time. Even though we have a daughter, Harriet, at school, there doesn't tend to be a rigid routine that enables me to describe my typical day. This is largely because of the nature of my work, but partly because I don't seem to find it easy to follow the general advice of separating work and home.

I work for a very small computer software house. There are currently two of us in the company full-time, although we take on contractors with specific skills as the needs arise. My colleague, who I have worked with for the last 22 years, works at the company's office in Mortlake. I occasionally go there for meetings, but usually I do my work either at home or at a client's site. To get to the office at Mortlake I usually drive – around the M25 and then the M4. I would rather go by public transport, but it would involve several trains and take far too long. If it's an important meeting I would allow an hour and a half by car, but if I'm lucky it only takes 45 minutes.

Whenever I am working away from home, it's always helpful to have my mobile phone with me. If I'm meeting up with my colleague before we attend a meeting somewhere, we can always let each other know if we've been held up and by how long. I also find it reduces the stress of trying to drive home, especially around the M25 when, because of the frequent traffic jams, it's not possible to guarantee an arrival time. Being able to say that I'm going to be 30 minutes late, for example, gives less to worry about.

Work-wise, 1999 has not been a typical year for me. A significant proportion of my work in 1999 has been for the Ford Motor Company. It has mainly been Y2K work – performing feasibility studies, making software changes and upgrades to plant-floor systems and performing tests to ensure that the systems will continue to operate in the new century.

At home I have a network of several computers (Alpha, VAX, Sun, PCs) running a mix of operating systems (VMS, Unix, NT and Windows 95/98). With these I can do most of the development work and testing, and only need to go to a client's site in order to set up testbeds on their network and install software over their network to computers throughout Europe and, in fact, the world.

I rely heavily on the internet for carrying out business and use it in four different ways. E-mail is my 'lifeline', although this has only been so for the last four years. Most of my 'discussions' are conducted by e-mail. I find it an excellent way to record decisions, etc., and to keep up-to-date. Every message I send to clients gets copied to my colleague and other consultants as appropriate and, similarly, their messages are copied to me. In this way, we avoid the need for frequent progress meetings because we are all constantly being kept aware of developments. E-mail attachments also play an important role. For example, I can send a draft of a design specification to a client in Germany, they can add their comments and I can re-issue the document the same day, copying it to all team members with no extra effort. And we are not just limited to documents as attachments. A colleague in Wales, for example, develops programs which he e-mails to me. I test and make my own contribution, e-mailing him the results for another iteration of updates. Finally, I take or e-mail the working program to the customer for installation.

As well as e-mail, the world-wide web is a very useful resource for business, particularly as a software developer. News groups can also be useful, especially with the time difference between the UK and the USA. I can post a query on a newsgroup in the late afternoon and first thing in the morning there will hopefully be lots of responses with suggestions for overcoming a particular problem. The fourth use of the internet is as a network. When authorized, I can connect over the internet to any other computer on the internet (for the cost of a local telephone call) and carry out software maintenance on that computer – investigating problems, uploading updates, etc.

In addition to our BT phone line, I also have two cable phone lines that I use for work. The use of these two lines varies. At the moment I combine normal phone calls and fax on one line and use the second line for connecting to the internet. I have very little use for fax nowadays. At one time, I used to use the second line for fax, but until recently the line was used by one of our contractors who worked from his home and dialled into my computer network, so it was more convenient to move the fax. The fax is handled by computer and the computer also acts as the answerphone. I think most people with a set-up like mine would use ISDN. Apart from being a more expensive option, I decided not to convert yet, hoping that the much faster option of cable modems would become available, but it doesn't seem to have done yet.

The cable company, Cable & Wireless, also supplies cable television. We have subscribed to the basic service, mainly in order to get a better reception than our loft aerial gives. Having been built about 100 years ago, I prefer not to disturb the chimneys by fixing an external aerial! With cable television, we get the five main channels (BBC1, BBC2, ITV, Channel 4 and Channel 5) and a few news and supplementary channels such as Sky News and BBC News 24. Digital television is just about to be made available by the cable company. Digital television became available through an aerial in 1999 (or was it the year before?)

We use one of the bedrooms in our house as a study and that is where I spend most of my time. Apart from school trips, as described below, I have little need to leave the house on a day when I am working at home. Occasionally I may need some stationery (when I've printed yet another manual that I've downloaded over the internet and realize I don't have a binder to put it in) and take a trip to Office World in Watford. But I can order, usually over the internet, most things I need and have them delivered. We are fortunate in having a postbox (a Victorian one set in the wall) outside our house. But its opening isn't very large, so I normally take a walk up to the village post office on the odd occasion when I need to post a letter (26p for first class).

I usually take and collect my daughter from school for the half of the week when my wife is working. If I am working away from home then we usually manage by my wife dropping Harriet off at a friend's on the way to work and arranging for Harriet to go to tea to a friend's after school. We then reciprocate or pay in 'baby sitting tokens'. Harriet goes to Divine Saviour School in Broomfield Rise. When the weather is fine and, more importantly, we are not late, we try to walk. It takes about 15 minutes, walking up Abbots Road, along the footpath, down Dellmeadow, past the field planted with trees (in 1993, I think), through the little wood and across the sports field. This brings us to Gallows Hill Lane, which is a very tricky road to cross at that time in the morning. The shortcut through the woods can be very muddy so then I resort to the car.

With interruptions during the day for school trips, odd domestic chores and perhaps the occasional hour or two in the garden, I don't work the standard 7½-hour day in one go. Much of my 'spare time' is spent with computers. I enjoy desktop publishing and there always seems to be the odd poster or booklet that I 'volunteer' for and I produce the local history society's twice-yearly Journal. So a typical day starts at about 9 in the morning and goes on to gone midnight. Somewhere in between I will have done at least an expected day's work, and watched a bit of television!

As well as using the internet for work, it is also a convenient way of buying some things for home use. It's great for buying books, CDs, and the sorts of things that we previously bought by mail order, such as children's clothes. I like it because you can usually keep track of the progress of your order. For a while we tried placing our Sainsbury's supermarket order over the internet. But the ordering process was painfully slow if you wanted to make many changes to a standard order or search for items. It was handy, though, if the only time available for thinking about food shopping was in the evening. I am looking forward to what should soon be dramatic improvements to internet access by the introduction of digital services.

My guess is that the general opinion is that computers are becoming too prevalent, but I always feel that they are, or at least their use is, still far under-rated. Being able to use a keyboard is a skill that tends to put people off information technology; perhaps we'll see a change soon with the introduction of WAP (wireless application protocol) phones which will provide access to the internet without the need for a computer. An ideal place to collect and disseminate information is a web site and it is my aim in 2000 to launch the Abbots Langley Local History Society web site.

A Day in my Life

Pauline Wadl

I got up at 7.15 am, the September sun shining in the bedroom, another hot day – 80°F. Had breakfast in the kitchen where it was cooler: cereal and fruit, bread and home made lemon marmalade and instant coffee, after feeding Candy the cat with tinned cat-food and a tiny drop of (semi-skimmed) milk.

Put a load of washing in the machine, and went upstairs to get dressed and washed. Joan telephoned, and at the same time the doorbell rang with Parcel Post delivery. I put the washing on the rotary line in the garden, and at 9.30 am telephoned Elizabeth to check if she was in, and went with the folder of notes on the August 10 Eclipse, and a poster advertising the next meeting of the "Take Time" church evening group, to put on the notice board in her front garden. She served "proper" (freshly ground and filtered) coffee and we chatted, and she asked me to write up notes of my day's activities!

Then I walked on to the village with four of her letters to post and met Wendy Jefford who was looking after her grandson and another little girl. I put another "Take Time" poster on the fence of the Abbots House with the drawing pins already there from previous notices, and delivered one to the St Lawrence Church Parish Office and another to the Abbots Langley Library. At the Library I returned one book and took out another, and bought a large-print book which they had rejected. I picked up a plastic carrier bag and several plastic bottles to put in our recycling bin. I posted Elizabeth's letters in the postbox outside the Sub-Post Office at the corner of Abbots Road, and went to Budgens the supermarket for a tin of corned beef. I saw Ethel Stockwell sitting on a seat at the bus stop, waiting for a local bus to take her home; she had a fall on her garden path and couldn't walk that far. Saw Wendy Jefford leaving the Manor House Playing fields to go home, and called in at Vera's a few doors away. Margaret, her helper, told me that Pat Richardson had had a fall again.

By noon, I had returned home and put another load in the washing machine and taken in the washing which had dried outside on the rotary line, fed the cat again, and had lunch which included tomatoes from the garden. Frank came home from visiting his Polish friend George in Luton, with a gift of cold beetroot soup in a jar. Finished George's crossword puzzle, and began to read my library book. At 1.30 I listened on the radio to "Brain of Britain" and at 2 pm I sewed linings into the bathroom curtains. At 3 pm Frank put up the white numbers "24" on the front of the house, and then he re-hung the bathroom curtains. At 3.30 we had a cup of tea and someone was mowing their lawn; the afternoon was hot and humid, and headachy. Dogs in a

Village shop! Budgens, February 2000. Photo: Reg Nice

neighbour's house were barking. Mothers were collecting their children from the school along the road.

At 5.30 pm we had dinner of cold soup, corned beef with potatoes and runner beans (home grown by a friend in the next village), followed by stewed damsons with yoghurt. We cleared the dishes ready to wash them up by hand.

Frank went out to a National Children's Home (charity) committee meeting in Watford while I watched most of the Promenade Concert on television being broadcast live from the Albert Hall in London. Sir Simon Rattle conducted the Vienna Philharmonia Orchestra for Beethoven's 6th Symphony, terrific. The audience were very hot, wearing minimal clothing and using their programmes to fan themselves while the orchestra were in jackets. Sir Simon Rattle removed his jacket and conducted in shirtsleeves and waistcoat.

I gave the cat her supper and locked up, and at 10.30 pm Frank came home. Son Andrew telephoned, and we went to bed with the windows open, with one sheet and blanket, at 80°F once more.

Household Appliances in 1999

Jean Nice

I wonder what home appliances future inhabitants of Abbots Langley will possess?

At home here in Abbots Road in 1999 we have an automatic washing machine – this is the second model we have had, replacing our twin-tub (that is, washing compartment with heater and agitator and an adjacent spin-dryer) in about 1986. Now, to facilitate drying clothes in bad weather, we have a very useful tumble dryer in a separate machine as well.

For cleaning carpets we have a cylinder "Electrolux" vacuum cleaner, which we prefer to the upright models also available.

Another indispensable item we have is our fridge-freezer, a standard three cubic feet capacity refrigerator, topped by a two cubic feet capacity deep-freezer cabinet.

High on the list of most people's essentials is a colour television. Ours is still a basic four-channel model with two BBC stations and two ITV (British Broadcasting Corporation, and Independent TeleVision), although one is beginning to hear of "digital" multi-channel sets and for some years some people have had the necessary adaptions for cable and satellite television. As well as this we have a small radio in the kitchen and an amplifier and music centre (with record player, CD/compact disc player and tape deck) in the dining room.

Like most households we have a telephone (with which we can reach almost anywhere in the world) but not yet a portable personal phone (known now as "mobiles") although these are becoming increasingly popular.

For cooking we have a double electric oven plus a separate gas hob, and to supplement this we have a microwave oven and an electric toaster. For food preparation we use an electric Kenwood Chef mixer.

Our complement of household appliances is completed by a hand-held hairdryer.

Village Photographers

Eve and Ken Durtnall, Shady Firs Gallery

It all started in 1957 when I was given a box camera as a birthday present. I was hooked. Over the years I took mainly pictures of the family on special occasions at home or on holiday. I even had a hand flash-gun for indoor shots. In time I went to London to live and work and took some shots of various scenes.

In 1960 I got married and my husband, Ken, gave me a 35 mm Agfa Silette as a wedding present. I was very proud of this. It took a long time to get used to using it, with a hand-held light meter. Ken also had the same camera, so we always had one at the ready.

We moved to Abbots Langley in 1966, and thinking back it is a shame we didn't take any local pictures then – we were mostly photographing our children growing up!

In 1982 I bought the Pentax MES (Camera of the Year) which has interchangeable lenses. I gradually built up my confidence and in 1983 started recording the Cubs and Scouts at their ceremonies and jumble sales. Being a member of St Lawrence Church I also began to record church activities which is now an ongoing activity, and the church collection now amounts to over 1,500 photos. As I helped at Leavesden Hospital with the Library and Annexe Shop run by the Red Cross, I soon recorded inside and outside of the hospital, now sadly gone. In November 1986 I took a photo of Mr and Mrs Miller's sweet shop just before they closed down – we'll never see the like again. Over the next few years I did a photographic survey of Abbots Langley.

My husband decided it was time to earn some money to pay for my hobby which was gaining momentum and in 1989 we booked a table at the Henderson Hall a few weeks before Christmas at the Flea Market which had stalls selling all sorts of goods. Our photos sold at £1.50 plus envelope, and were most popular. And so Shady Firs Photography was born.

After trying our hand at weddings and pony club shows we

Eve's 1957 box camera. Photo: Eve Durtnall, 2000

decided to expand out of Abbots Langley by marketing our views of churches, pubs and views of Hertfordshire, Bedfordshire, Buckinghamshire and Middlesex at outlets further afield. The Abbots Langley Villager newspaper came out and I was then able to show the latest newsworthy pictures. It is great fun, as we get invited to many functions, clubs, schools and churches, for family and social occasions, and record events for posterity. Ken takes the views and I take the people and folk are very eager to get in the photo if I am around. This year, 2000, is busy as there are many special events taking place and I have now progressed to a Nikon F60 – all bells and whistles!

I expect we will still be clicking away when we are in our dotage. It's just something we both love doing.

A Day in My Life, September 1999

Anne Flanders

I awoke to a beautiful day, blue skies, a pleasant change after the heavy rain of the last few days.

Today being Tuesday, there's no need to rush as I have no early schedule to meet. After a leisurely breakfast of cereal, toast and marmalade, I turned my hand to the ironing while my husband, Geoffrey, put the breakfast crockery and cutlery into the dishwasher. Ironing I find to be quite a chore so I was glad when it was finished and put away into the airing cupboard.

Now for something much more interesting: my patchwork and quilting group meeting at 10 am. There are fourteen members in our group, and we meet twice a month in one another's houses. Today I was collected by my friend Linda and taken in her car to Dorothy's house, she lives just outside Berkhamsted in most beautiful countryside. Her garden looked a picture in the autumn sunshine, red apples glowed on the trees and her hanging baskets were still full of colour. Our guest speaker was Sheila Acton, who is an Area Representative for the Quilters Guild. She gave us a brief history and a lot of information about the Guild, and she also told us about the City and Guilds course that she had just completed in Patchwork and Quilting. She brought along quite a lot of her work which was most exquisite.

I arrived home about 1 pm and after a sandwich lunch with Geoffrey I drove into Watford to meet a friend at the swimming pool. We go once a week and enjoy half-an-hour's lane swimming and then a bubble and chat in the spa.

I returned home feeling very refreshed and after a cup of tea got ready to do two hours of work at our local Health Centre where I am a Practice Nurse. I saw about eight patients, doing various tasks, for example ear syringing, holiday vaccinations, dressings. I enjoy my work, only now working a few hours a week as I will be retiring next year. I have worked at the Health Centre for over twenty-five years, and have seen many changes. Our premises have been enlarged over the years and we now have a wonderful building. Our treatment rooms are very spacious, and quite different to the tiny room I started off in which had no windows or storage space. We now have a new computer system, replacing quite an old system of ten years ago. We have a ten-minute appointment system for most patients, but have double appointments for lengthy dressings and minor surgery which is performed by the doctor.

My evening finished at 7 pm, and I drove home and had supper and a chat with Geoffrey, and then he drove off to Harpenden where he is rehearsing with the local Operatic Society for their performance of "Carousel" in two weeks time.

I relaxed into an armchair doing my quilting and watching television – the end of a very pleasant day.

Abbots Langley Belfry Records of Events from Midsummer 1899

John Sutton, Tower Secretary

"Abbots Langley – Belfry, Record of Events from Mid-Summer 1899" *is a black-bound book, approximately seven inches by nine inches, passed to me by the Tower Captain, David Harris. With gaps, it covers the period up to 1935, giving in some cases quite detailed accounts of events. Meetings, outings, dinners, and cricket and quoit matches against the choir are some of the items featured. Naturally, ringing takes up the majority of entries: for marriages, for deaths, for peace, for the King, for the Queen (Victoria) and of course for services. Also, the members of the tower are listed. The current diary was started in 1984, and sadly the current crop of ringers do not include "sports and social" as part of the membership of the* *tower, compared with the entries of the early twentieth century, and thus generally the inclusion of non-ringing events is by exception. Here follows the entries for 1899 and 1900, and the comments made in the year 2000 are in italics.*

1899

Abbots Langley Parish Church Belfry: President, Revd A H Parnell; Foreman, Mr W D Kentish; Deputy Foreman, Mr E Mansfield; Bellringer, Mr W Baldwin; Bellringer, Mr G Crawley; Bellringer, Mr A Barr; Hon Secretary, Mr E Glenister; Probationer, Mr A Dowse; Probationer, Mr E Ridgeway.
No ladies. No children. Currently our tower membership of seventeen includes four ladies and three children.

A cricket match was played on ..... between the Bellringers and Choir of the Abbots Langley Parish Church, on the Manor House Cricket Ground. The Vicar playing on the ringers side. The scores at the finish were: ..... Bellringers, ... Choir.
Unfortunately, no scores were given for either of these matches.

Annual Trip: On Saturday ..... the vicar *(Revd Parnell)* very kindly took the ringers by brake to Ivanhoe, Bucks, and in addition the Ivinghoe ringers were entertained to lunch at the Town Hall. The vicar presided at one table and the Revd T Harvey, vicar of Ivinghoe, at the other. After lunch the ringers of each parish gave a merry peal on the church bells. A game at cricket and several games at quoits all ending in favour of the visitors ended the very enjoyable visit; except the drive home which was reached about 11 pm.
Not dated but thought to be in August from the other entries of this annual event. Ivanhoe is presumed to be Ivinghoe. The brake was probably a four wheeled carriage which could carry up to eight persons. As Ivinghoe is about fifteen miles away this would have taken about three hours compared with less than half an hour by motor car today. (Does anyone know the rules of Quoits?)

St Lawrence's
Abbots Langley

1900
Ladysmith

On Thursday March 1st the bellringers rang a merry peal which lasted one hour and ten minutes in commemoration of the Relief of Ladysmith which was officially announced that day. Members present: Messrs W D Kentish, E Mansfield, W Baldwin, E Glenister, G Crawley, A Barr and A Dowse.

Relief of Mafeking

On May 19th the bellringers met at 3 pm and rang a merry peal, which lasted till 4.30 pm without a stop, and also at night another was given which was started at 9 pm and finished in commemoration of the relief of Mafeking, which siege had lasted 216 days. Members present: Messrs E Mansfield, W D Kentish, W Baldwin, E Glenister, A Barr, A Dowse and T Chalk (sub).

Fall of Pretoria

On Whit Tuesday the news reached the village that Pretoria had been occupied by Her Majesty's Troops. The ringers met and rang a merry peal which lasted 40 minutes. Present: Messrs Mansfield, Chalk, Dowse, Barr, Baldwin and C Harris sub.

Fortunately, we only ring for Remembrance Day (11 November) when we remember all those who died during the two World Wars (1914–1918 and 1939–1945).

Mr W D Kentish

A Meeting of the bellringers held in the belfry on Monday May 21st, the vicar being present, when Mr W D Kentish tendered his resignation which was accepted with regret. Mr Parnell expressed his regret of himself and the ringers in losing so valuable a member, who took such an active part in the work, and the vicar wishing Mr Kentish health and prosperity in his new home at Windsor. Mr Dowse proposed and Mr Barr seconded, that Mr E Mansfield be Foreman Ringer which was accepted. Mr Glenister proposed and Mr Dowse seconded that Mr W Baldwin be Deputy Foreman which was also accepted.

David Harris is currently our "Tower Captain".

Inside St Lawrence's bell tower, 1991. Photo: Eve Durtnall

Queen's Birthday

On Thursday morning at 5 am May 24th a peal was given to celebrate Her Majesty's Birthday, and also in the evening before and after the service a similar peal was rung...

Note the time! Probably this was before they went to work on the local farms which would start very early at this time of the year. The earliest we ring now is at eight forty-five for Service.

Marriage of Revd G N Emmett

On Wednesday June 20th 1900 at St Peter's Church Ealing the marriage of Revd G N Emmett and Miss Elise/Elsie Gurning took place. The ringers of Abbots Langley church rang a long merry peal which lasted one hour and ten minutes in the evening to celebrate the above.

Home Coming of Revd and Mrs Emmett

The ringers gave another peal which lasted one hour and ten minutes, on the homecoming of the above. The Revd and Mrs Emmet, coming to the belfry, tendered their thanks to the ringers for their trouble and kindness. Present: Messrs Mansfield, Baldwin, House, Barr, Glenister and C Harris, sub.

Cricket Match

A match was played at Langley House, by kind permission of R Henty Esq who was present with the Misses Henty. The vicar and Mrs Parnell very kindly provided tea for the players which were the bellringers v choir. The thanks of each team were accorded to the Revd and Mrs Parnell for their kindness, also to the other ladies for their kind assistance.

Bellringers 47 and 21, against the choir 52 and 58.

Quoits

A quoit match was played in the vicarage meadow (by kind permission of Revd A H Parnell) between the bellringers and choir on August 13th 1900 which resulted in a win for the ringers by 4 games to one. Scores (choir first) E Mansfield 22 v W Baldwin 5;

H T Atkingson 6 v A Dowse 21; C Hawkshaw 5 v D White 11; T Thatcher 8 v E Glenister 21; W Botwright 12 v T Chalk 21; total overall 63 v 79.

The choir appear to have a "ringer" playing for them in Mr Mansfield! (A pun on the word "ringer" which nowadays also means "an illegal player". Mr Mansfield was recently elected Foreman Ringer!)

Visit to Ivanhoe Ringers August 18 1900

The Ringers of Abbots Langley with the Rev Parnell met the Ivanhoe Ringers with the Rev Harvey at Ashridge Monument and through the kindness of the Rev & Mrs Parnell were entertained to lunch and tea, a game of Cricket and Quoits were also played. The Cricket match ended in Abbots Langley Ringers favour, 118 for six wickets against 75 all out. The game at Quoits was in favour of Ivanhoe by 6 games to 3.

The Late Duke of Edinburgh

An Half Muffled Peal took place on ..... on account of the Death of the Duke of Saxe-Coburg, the Peal lasted 40 minutes. Present Mr E Mansfield (Foreman) Messrs Dowse, Baldwin, Bar, Glenister & T Chalk (sub).

Mr W Rance & Others

On Monday August 28th, at a meeting held in the Belfry, in the presence of the Vicar and the Bellringers, Mr W Rance was appointed to a full Bellringer and Mr Evans and Mr D White were appointed Probationers.

Nowadays, we are affiliated to the Hertford County Association of Change Ringers (HCA). The rules of that Society stipulate that members are Probationers unless they can ring 120 changes inside or 500 changes behind on the tenor bell.

Marriage of Mr W Evans

On Tuesday October 30, the Ringers met together and rang a

merry Peal which lasted 55 minutes on occasion of the Homecoming of Mr and Mrs Evans after their Marriage which took place
in Kent on October 27th. Present, Messrs E Mansfield, Dowse,
Baldwin, Barr, Glenister, and D White.

Boer War
Return of Private J Puddifoot December 6th. The Safe Return from
the Front of Mr J Puddifoot, Private in the Army Reserves brought
the Ringers together on Thursday night who rang a peal which
lasted 45 minutes.

This completes the entries for 1899–1900.

A Day in the Life of a Church Administrator

Pam Rastall

The Parish Church of St Lawrence, Abbots Langley and Bedmond

The walk up the hill from my home to St Lawrence Church in
the centre of the village, takes about fifteen minutes. I head
straight for the Vicarage to arrive at 9.00 am. The Vicar, Canon
Brian Andrews, and I then spend about thirty minutes looking at
the post, dealing with the previous day's or evening's queries,
checking diaries, discussing meetings, etc.

At 9.30 am I go to the Church Office, which is part of the
Church Hall built in 1965. The first thing I do is listen to the
messages on the answerphone: these could include bookings for
weddings or baptisms, enquiries about services, or maybe
someone who wants to speak to the Vicar.

Today, the date being Wednesday 22nd March 2000, I had a few mums (yes, it's usually the mums) to phone to confirm or discuss dates for the baptism of their babies. Most baptisms are booked for 3.00 pm on a Sunday afternoon and we often arrange two at the same service. There are about 80 baptisms a year in St Lawrence most of which take place between April and September.

I also had two couples to phone about their weddings: one to check the date of a rehearsal before their wedding next month, the other to book a date for a meeting with the Vicar as they would like to marry here in 2001. The wedding season is just beginning and there are 32 booked through to the end of September this year.

A phone call from the local undertaker means a booking for a funeral for next week. A check with the Vicar first to make sure he is available at the appointed time, then a return call to the undertaker to obtain details of the deceased and the next-of-kin. The clergy (and there are three of them at present: two full-time and one retired) conduct about 80 funerals between them each year, most of which take place at the local crematorium in Garston, with maybe a dozen of them taking place in St Lawrence Church.

Visitors to the Office might include: somebody to look at the gravestones in the churchyard as they are researching their family tree; one of the clergy from another church in the village; someone who comes in for a chat about something which is bothering them (and we try not to turn them away as pastoral care is a significant part of the work of the Church Office); a pupil wanting information about the church for a school project; a mother wanting details about activities provided by the church for her children – the list is endless, and it's not always 'church' related but we do aim to help as many as we can.

Lunchtime – well, by law I have to take a break, so I lock the door and pull down the blind for an hour. Not as many people visit or phone in the afternoon, so often I have time to type up minutes of meetings or reports without too many interruptions.

No two days are the same and what I plan to do first thing in the morning is often not accomplished by last thing at night because something more urgent (or interesting!) has cropped up. My working day officially finishes at 5.30 pm but sometimes I have to stay to finish a service sheet for a funeral the next day or for a Sunday service – there are often deadlines to make. Then I head home down the hill and put on the kettle!

A Day in My Life – November 1999

Dr Richard Simons

I woke up at 6.45 am feeling stiff after spending Sunday afternoon up a ladder in the garden. My four-year old son, George, clambered into bed with me as Anne got up to go to work. Once in his school uniform, George sat in front of the television while I prepared our breakfast of hot porridge. At 7.45 am Anne left to drive to Hemel Hempstead station where she caught the train to work in London. George and I left home at 8.10 am and found the car nearby was out of petrol. So we had to go to Bedmond to fill up before driving to Boxmoor to drop George at school by 8.30 am. I then set off for my work at HR Wallingford. The old car I have bought for this daily trip along the Icknield Way does not have a radio, so there is plenty of time for personal thoughts – of the view, of activities at home, and the work ahead. This morning's journey was delayed more than usual by a slow-moving Land Rover with a trailer.

I am on secondment from University College London (UCL) for six months, finding out how consulting engineers operate – with the objective of enhancing my future teaching of undergraduates. On arrival at the Wallingford offices at 9.35 am I found the room I share with two colleagues empty: one of them (who is looking forward to retiring in a year or two) arrived at 9.50 am and the other was taking a few days holiday to visit York. The company works a "flexitime" system where staff can arrive any time between 8 am and 10 am and leave between 4 pm and 6.30 pm, taking lunch between 12 noon and 2 pm. Staff are expected to average seven and a half hours per day over a month, and any excess time worked can be redeemed as "flexi-days" leave.

Having taken the last week off to look after George during half term, it took half an hour to deal with my incoming e-mail messages. These were a mix of HR administration, information relating to on-going projects, and UCL work. At 10.15 am I was called by a telephone salesman and asked for the week's coffee order for the UCL Academic Staff Common Room (of which I remain Secretary – and responsible for keeping the coffee machines stocked). Immediately afterwards, I received another telephone call, this time from the architect retained by St Lawrence Church, Abbots Langley. He wished to discuss various conservation projects planned for the church, in particular the erosion of mortar on the West Tower, damage to the clunch stone, and repair of a small blind window. He also promised to complete plans for the extension to the Citizens Advice Bureau housed in the old stable block behind the church within a couple of days.

At 10.45 am I got down to some real work – reviewing a technical paper describing a supposedly novel form of coastal defence for the editorial board of Nature magazine. This required me to refer to textbooks in the company library. The review was typed on my desktop personal computer, and sent off to the editor by e-mail (printing a paper copy for my own file). Went for lunch (stew and dumplings) in the canteen at 12.15 pm with a table of colleagues all keen to discuss the Rugby World Cup semi-finals.

After lunch I had a meeting with the HR Wallingford Equipment Salesman to discuss another project with which I am involved. In this case, we are developing an economic method of absorbing the unwanted backwash waves that are produced behind the company's proprietary wave generators. I had already conducted some tests at UCL in my own wave tank, and we needed to plan the next phase of tests for the larger tanks at HR. The afternoon was punctuated by discussions with colleagues on various ongoing projects that posed interesting problems, particularly concerning silting up of two harbours in Ireland and the erosion of a golf course in Norfolk. Just before leaving for home at 6.35 pm I had a meeting with an old friend who was visiting from Liverpool to discuss the possible establishment of a national network of university researchers interested in Coastal Engineering.

It was dark when I left Wallingford, and there was heavy traffic all the way. The hold-up for road works at Hunton Bridge was the last straw and I got home at 7.30 pm. George and Anne were watching "A Bug's Life" (a Disney video) and we had supper soon after. Anne had made a cottage pie from Sunday lunch leftovers, and the apple ginger was excellent. George then did some picture colouring by numbers and reluctantly went to bed at 9.30 pm. Before going to sleep, he read his homework book and I tested him on his "flashcards".

At 10 pm I prepared a poster on my home computer to advertise a local "Christmas Dinner" and then typed two letters. Started to proof-read a technical report written for me by a research assistant at UCL, and retired to bed at 12.30 am when too tired to concentrate!

The Pocket Watch

Sue and Dave Noise

A couple of years ago I was given a pocket watch. Etched on the back was a caricature of a man with a big nose and dressed in a high crumpled hat. Beneath the face was engraved the name "A. Sloper". On the inside of the case was engraved "Ally Sloper's Half Holiday".

Sue, my wife, and I thought we would try and find out about this watch so we went along to the Abbots Langley Library. We had thought that possibly the caricature could have been that of a music hall entertainer so requested any books on the subject.

They had nothing in stock, but the librarian said she would check at Watford for us. I received a call the following week but there was no luck and over the next two or three weeks hope faded.

Suddenly, however, on returning from a few days in York, there was a letter awaiting which I opened immediately. It contained the name and phone number of a gentleman who is the historian of the British Music Hall Society, so I phoned him up straight away. He asked what my interest was, and informed me that Ally Sloper was in fact a cartoon character and not a real person, from a Victorian Magazine called "Ally Sloper's Half Holiday" and that he had a copy from 1886 which I could study. This I received a few days later, thus solving my problem as to who Ally Sloper actually was. All I need to know now is who may have owned the watch.

I have to thank the staff of Abbots Langley Library for the diligence with which they applied themselves. This seemed to us to be a service over and above the normal function of issuing books etc., and one for which we are most grateful.

The Library Service is one we must preserve, defend and promote whenever necessary, and perpetuate it into the next millennium for all those who follow us.

Abbots Langley Bowling Club

Archives provided by John Sutton

The formation of the Bowling Club in the 1930s is covered by the following letter and poem. The letter was the result of a request for information at the time of the Bowling Club's Golden

Bowling Club 60th Anniversary, 1990. Photo: Eve Durtnall

Jubilee in 1980. A commemorative card issued for the jubilee states:

"In the 1920s a tennis court in a Trowley Rise Garden was used for Bowls practice until permission was given for practice on the Cricket ground, with matches played away, although a few matches were played on the lawn of the Manor House.

"The Abbots Langley Bowling Club was formed at a meeting held in 1930. The present green was purchased in 1933 when five trustees paid £12 each to make up the required £60. The green was opened by Major and Mrs J H Drake on the 31st May 1935. The Parish Council took over the green in 1960 and the Club became their tenants.

"The Club has provided the Watford & District Bowling Association with Presidents: J Barr (1950), R Smith (1967), F Herbert (1976) and in 1974 Mrs V Rollings was President of the Watford & District Ladies Bowling Association."

The letter from Jim Barr (1950 President) to Vic Lythaby in 1976:

12 River Close
Wimbourne Minster
Dorset
BH21 1DN

12 October 1976

Dear Vic,

Your letter has caused me some sort of shock and it has caused me to put on my thinking cap. I can, however, give you a brief history of the Club, but naturally after all this time, I cannot remember precise dates.

The Bowling Club owes its origin to the Abbots Langley Social Club which was in existence in the 1920s, following the 1914–18 War. One of the functions of the Social Club was the arranging of char-a-banc (now coach) trips to places of interest within easy distance. One of these trips went to Little Gaddesden where the party stopped for refreshment at the Bridgewater Arms, at the rear of which was a strip of turf on which some locals were rolling up woods.

Some of the Action men thought it would be a good idea if they did something similar and as a result a few started rolling up woods on the tennis court of Mr D H Prangnell in Trowley Rise.

Subsequently, others became interested and it was evident that Mr Prangnell's lawn could not accommodate all and it was then decided to form a club, the leading lights being DH Prangnell, Arthur Flint (builder), Bert Lowe and Fred Hince (Maintenance Staff at Leavesden Hospital), Fred Ginger (Deputy Head Attendant at the hospital) and W S May (Head Gardener at the Manor House) then occupied by the Ward Family. The Ward family owned all the field between their garden and the farm, and the Cricket Club used their present pitch by grace and favour of Mr Ward.

When the Club was formed, Mr May became the first Secretary and he was able to induce his boss (Mr Ward) to allow the bowlers to practise on the cricket table, the Cricket Club having no objection. Furthermore, Mr Ward allowed the Club to arrange a few friendly matches on the lawn on the terrace in front of the Manor House.

Subsequently, it was thought something more permanent was required and a firm of Watford Builders (two brothers, one of whom was a member of the Herts Bowling Club) who built the estate bordering High Street, Chapel Road and the Crescent found they could not use a piece of ground, which is now the Bowling Green, the only access to which being from the footpath linking Chapel Road to Trowley Bottom. The Club had little or no cash so the Founder Members agreed to subscribe shares to enable the land to be purchased for £70 (if my memory serves me right).

By this time Mr May had died and Mr Ward had moved away from the Manor House, the new occupant being Major Drake. Major Drake became President of the Club and the principle officers then were D H Prangnell – Secretary, F Ginger – Treasurer; and A Flint – Chairman of the Committee. We then set about making the green, levels being taken by D H Prangnell and H Lowe. We then prepared the ditches which we drained into the public footpath ditch. As water was required, the Water Co provided a supply from a meter in Chapel Road, the supply pipe also running along the ditch in the public footpath.

The green was completed (I think) in 1934 and was opened by Major Drake. Following this a match was played against the Herts Bowling Club, Watford. (Matches with the Herts Club continued for some years – all at Abbots, the Watford professors always looked upon the Abbots Club in those days as their "Daughter".)

There was no pavilion and the ladies brewed tea on a "Primus" stove in a galvanised shed which we erected at the entrance from the public footpath. I think we were affiliated to the Herts County and the Watford & District Bowling Associations in the following year. Affiliation to the Watford & District Association was contingent upon the

Club being affiliated to the County. I do not know who is querying the 1932 date but I feel sure that it is right.

The Pavilion was erected <u>at cost</u> by Mr Ernie Jones (a member and a Master Builder) and the whole of the cost was covered by the Ladies, who raised money by holding jumble sales, whist drives etc. I imagine this came into use in the 1935 or 1936 season.

In 1936 we had new officers. I took over the Secretaryship, Mr F Daisley (Newsagent in the High Street) was Treasurer, Mr Flint carried on as Chairman of the Committee. About this time Major Drake left the Manor House, and Mr Alan East of Greenways was elected as President.

Mr Frank Roberts (one time Manager of the Palace Theatre, Watford) a member of the Club from its outset was President of the Watford & District Bowling Association throughout the 1939/45 War years and though he was elected to that position as a member of the Herts Bowling Club, he can be considered as the first President of the Association from the Abbots Langley Club. I was the next in 1950.

The entrance from Chapel Road was purchased for (I think) £250 before 1939 and was part of a parcel on which the Scouts had an option and which they eventually found they did not need.

I gave up the Secretaryship at the end of 1955 consequent upon my removal to Potten End and was succeeded by Mr Cyril Ginger, to whom all records, minute books, etc. were handed over.

The Title Deeds, and such relevant documents, were never in my possession and were presumably held by the Bank or the Solicitor who acted for the Club. These would include the Trust Deed which was drawn up when the Founder Members decided to forgo their interests and set up the trust. The documents are now presumably in the hands of the Local Authority to whom the green was subsequently handed over by the then Trustees. This was after my time.

I believe the road to which I have referred to as Chapel Road is now known as Langley Road.

This is the best I can do and I hope it will be of interest. With all best wishes, hoping you all Winter well,

Yours sincerely,

Jim Barr

I have not mentioned the Ladies Club which was formed in 1938.

***

The following poem was written in 1930 by Mr W S May (the Club's first Secretary) as a preface to the first Minute Book. *Mine host at the Royal Oak was Mr Follett, who whilst not on the committee (no doubt due to the pressures of running the Royal Oak) was an active supporter of the Club.*

In the year 1930
On a night somewhat dirty.
Two or three members of the club
were taking refreshment in a pub.
Don't be alarmed, they were not there for a soak.
But just to take shelter beneath the Royal Oak.

After a while in came a member of the Cricket Club
not having much to spend having just paid his sub
after a general talk
the night being too wet for a walk.

The cricketer after being treated to something nourishing
mentioned the finances of his club were not flourishing.
It was then generally agreed
if the club was in need...
We old men of the village would set the ball rolling
by forming a club of our own and start bowling.
In return for the use of the Cricket Ground
we would help their finances by a whip round.

After much heart burning and talk
and seeing no way our proposal to baulk.
A letter was sent to Major Drake
asking for the use of his ground for the old men's sake.
Major Drake's reply was as you know,
a very hearty welcome and hope the club would well go.

A committee was formed with a Flint at the head
no one will be so (Lowe) as to (Barr) us now he said.
With a Britton and Parson.

In the year 1932
Let's see what we can do.
And if any outsider is hard to convince
let him have a word with Dazely, Prangnell, Halsey and Hince.

The ground that we play on is not level.
If anyone complains, let him go to the devil.

We have amongst our members a chemist, and in fact two.
So don't feel afraid to join, you will never feel blue.
I am sure that one or the other will kill or cure you.

A plumber, a carpenter and clerk
So if we want any rolling done they get on with the work.

We want more fixtures
We are open to play any sort of mixtures.

Some of our members it is true play best in the dark.
Often when there is money to be earned, so you can quite
see their lark.
With matches they singe the hair of the Jack,
to coax him to bring them luck, and their money back!

We play for the love of the game,
and not to advertise our power, and make cheap fame.
The members of the club are not that sort,
and it's well known that everyone is a sport.

We played and we lost to the great firm of Wander
I guess when we play there again they shall have reason to ponder.
Rink two it is true
on this occasion had reason to feel blue.
The next time we played them and looked like winning,
when someone bribed the clerk of the weather with a shilling.

"This is an absolutely true record of how the Bowling Club originated. WSM."

A Day in My Life, March 2000

Simon Stanley

I am sixteen-years old and live in Abbots Langley. I have lived here all my life. I wake up at about 7 am and have eaten breakfast by about 7.45, and I have to cycle to school so I leave at about 8 o'clock to call for a friend. We arrive at school at about 8.30 and school starts at 8.45. I go to Parmiter's mixed school and have great fun there. The day starts with registration or assembly until about 9.05 and then the lessons start. Lessons at our school are thirty-five minutes long with a break at 10.50 until 11.10, and lunch is at 12.55 until 1.50. On a Monday and Friday school ends at about 3.10 pm but on the rest of the week it ends at 3.45.

I am in year eleven, and this means I am taking my GCSEs *[General Certificate of Secondary Education]* this year. I have had to choose to drop certain subjects and to continue with others. Many of the subjects I am taking are compulsory and so we had no choice in the matter. Here is my timetable:

	lesson 1	lesson 2	lesson 3		lesson 4	lesson 5	lesson 6		lesson 7	lesson 8	lesson 9
M	English	English	Maths	B	Maths	Chemistry	Physics	L	Games	Games	
T	Biology	Biology	Spanish	R	Spanish	Art	Art	U	Form Period	Chemistry	Chemistry
W	Games		Resistant Materials	E	Technology	Maths	Art	N	Biology	History	History
Th	PSHE	RS	English	A	English	Spanish	Spanish	C	Maths	Art	Art
F	English	English	History	K	History	Information	Studies	H	Physics	Physics	

My favourite day is Wednesday because we have double Technology and History. In History we have to learn about the two World Wars, the Peace Treaties, Germany and the Weimar Republic, Hitler, America in the 1920s and the Cold War. The only thing I do not like about Wednesdays is that we have Maths. I do not like Maths very much, I am in the intermediate set which means I can only get a "B" grade. The subject that makes up for Maths is Biology. I like this subject a lot and hope to take it in the Sixth Form. I am starting to worry about my exams.

The first exam is my Art exam, this is only two weeks away and my Spanish Orals are only three weeks away. The rest of the exams are after Easter, when we have stood down. This is only a week after Easter, leaving us a week of study leave before the first exam. If I get good enough grades, I hope to go to Sixth Form and hopefully on to university. The new A-level system means I have to take four exams the first year, drop a subject and then take three more exams the following year. I hope to do English, History, Biology and Product Design-Technology.

On Tuesday lunchtime I play in a music band called Concert Band. We play in many school functions and also play a Christmas Concert at Breakspeare School. I play the French Horn and there are three other people in the section. We all have a lot of fun and enjoy it a lot.

After school I do several things. On Tuesdays I have my music lesson from 7.30 until 8 o'clock. On Thursdays I have a trampolining club that I go to with some friends at school. On Saturday I work in the mornings and play hockey for West Herts

Hockey Club in the afternoon, and I also play hockey on Sunday mornings. So I have quite a busy week, but not compared to some of my friends.

Money, Weights and Measures

Elizabeth Manning

At school in the 1930s, 40s and 50s I found figures difficult to master. Had I known the word then I might have thought I was numerically 'dyslexic'. My ineptitude at anything to do with numbers was, I was told, due to laziness! Looking back, though, I think I would have mastered my sums in a more competent way using metric and decimal systems rather than pounds/shillings/ pence and pounds/ounces/stones. Incidentally, nowadays everyone is allowed to use a tiny pocket-sized calculator for the simplest of sums, and that too would have helped me enormously with my arithmetic!

In 1901 one bought things with pounds, shillings and pence, and three-farthings, and halfpennies (known as ha'pence or ha'pennies) and farthings. There were also nice little silver threepenny bits, silver sixpences, florins, half-crowns, crowns, and sovereigns. Paper money came in ten-shilling notes, pound notes, five pound notes.

There were twenty shillings to the pound; twelve pence to a shilling; two shillings made a florin; two shillings and sixpence made a half-a-crown, and five shillings made a crown. Twenty-one shillings made a guinea, and a sovereign was a gold coin worth exactly one pound. Four farthings made one penny, and two ha'pennies made a penny.

There had even been a small coin called a groat but I never saw one. Imagine adding up the bill in a shop with all those little divisions of a pound, and getting the change right – no tills which did the sums for you and told you the change to give if you keyed in the amount tendered! Until the late sixties and seventies everything was paid for with cash; cheques and credit cards gradually became acceptable and now one can almost manage without a heavy pocketful of coins. To open a bank account in Abbots Langley and to pay in and draw out cash was only a problem if you forgot the time because the opening hours were quite restricted, and there were, of course, no Automatic Transaction Machines on the wall outside!

Goods were weighed in avoirdupois weight, that is in pounds, ounces – sixteen of which made one pound – and fourteen pounds made one stone.

Sixteen drachms made one ounce; 28 pounds made one quarter; four quarters made one hundredweight (cwt), and twenty hundredweight made one ton. Eight stones also made one hundredweight, as did 112 pounds.

When I left school in the fifties I weighed seven stone ten pounds. You don't need to know what I weigh now, but I still register it in stones and pounds, as I cannot readily visualise my weight made up entirely of pounds, it sounds too much.

Dry measure for larger quantities of goods such as flour, corn, and so on, were also measured in gallons!

Two gallons made one peck; four pecks made a bushel; eight bushels made one quarter, three bushels equalled one bag and four bushels made one coomb. 36 bushels equalled one chaldron, and 40 bushels equalled one wey (a horse-load), two weys equalled one last.

All the village grocers, greengrocers, butchers, bakeries and the fishmonger had scales to weigh their goods from large bins or sacks or trays; the shop assistants had quickly to work out the price of a quarter of a pound of sugar from the stated cost of one pound of sugar, add it to the rest of the purchases of little portions of bacon or cheese or flour parcelled up, and there were no calculators and one did not serve yourself in the shop. Behind the counters were people who I admired tremendously; they could do sums of such complexity so quickly I could never check whether they were correct!

Reg Cooper, retired coal merchant, 1988. Photo: Eve Durtnall

Our coal was delivered to Follett Drive from Mr Reg Cooper's coal yard in Popes Road. We had built large concrete bunkers in our back garden and needed them filled regularly to keep the boiler and fire going during winter. Everyone bought coal, we all had coal bunkers in our gardens. In London it was delivered down a special round shute into the cellar – many pavements in London still have small round iron covers over the coal shute which were the coal merchant's advertisement. Coal fires and boilers were in every house and the coal merchant's horse and cart or lorry was a fine sight with a distinctive smell.

The coal measures started at 14 pounds for one stone, twenty-eight pounds equalled one quarter and so on, and were the same as in the avoirdupois table, with the addition of one sack equalling one hundredweight, but one large sack equalled two hundredweight.

Our purchase of 1 cwt of coal was a regular, necessary and major expenditure in the sixties with three young children, and we used to pay Mrs Cooper in her little office at the rear of their house which was opposite the baby clinic, where our little darlings were carefully weighed by the Health Visitors in pounds and ounces.

Liquid goods came in gills, half pints, pints, quarts (two pints) and gallons, still fairly familiar in 1999.

Four gills made one pint, and four quarts made one gallon, although in the north of England one gill was equal to half a pint of liquid, and a noggin was a quarter pint. Nine gallons was one firkin **(now you know what the pub sign signifies)** *and ten gallons equal one anker. Two firkins was one kilderkin, and two kilderkins was one barrel; one and a half barrels was a hogshead, and two hogsheads made one butt, and two butts made – one tun.* **So now you know the meaning of the other pub sign!**

Fluid ounces complicated the issue: they were used in cookery recipes, at 20 fluid ounces to the pint. Everyone had milk delivered to the doorstep every day, there were pint bottles, half-pint bottles, and little bottles of yoghurt too, and in Follett Drive, as in the rest of the village, there was great competition for customers with the Express, Co-op and Braziers dairies competing for our orders.

To measure distances there was long measure and land measure, square measure, cubic measure and even nautical measure – although in Abbots Langley the latter was not used much! For long measure we used miles, yards, feet and inches plus a host of other measures: three feet made a yard, and twelve inches equalled a foot; these measurements were originally based on the human figure; horses are still measured in hands, that is four inches equalling a hand, and three inches being a palm.

Three barleycorns equal one inch, two and a half inches equal one nail. Nine inches equal one span (of a hand); eighteen inches equal one cubit. While five feet equalled one geometric pace, a military pace equalled two and a half feet. Rods, poles and perches, chains and furlongs and leagues also entered the sums: five and a half yards equal one pole or rod; four poles (or 22 yards) equal one chain; 40 poles equal one furlong; eight furlongs equal one mile – which may be more familiar to people in 1999 as 1,760 yards!

Land measure used to be made up of a link which equalled 7.92 inches; 25 links made a pole or rod; 100 links made one chain and eighty chains made a mile. **Square measure** included links, square poles, square chains, and acres and they all had to be remembered with their equivalents, and then one barony was forty hides, and one hide was 100 acres – shades of Domesday Book here. Forty square poles equalled one rood; four roods made one acre and 640 acres equalled one square mile. Finally there was a cord foot which was sixteen cubic feet, and eight cord feet which equalled one cord. A rod or a pole or a perch equalled thirty and a quarter square yards, I cannot possibly think who needed such an odd measurement.

On the original plan for our home at Stonehaven, Greenways, drawn by Bert Flint in 1926 for his uncle George Flint to build the house for himself, all the measurements are of course in feet and inches; Bert's son, Roger, presented the drawing to us when he discovered it in a drawer after Bert died. It is a treasured possession, framed, and admired as it now hangs in our hall.

Of course, not all these units were in everyday use. By the 1940s, we measured length in feet, inches, yards and miles, and liquid in pints, gallons and fluid ounces; weight was measured in pounds, ounces, stones, hundredweight and tons, and area in square feet, square yards and acres. Nonetheless, in school the old tables applied, presumably to keep us quiet and teach us numeracy.

Can you imagine the complexities of arithmetic with all that to master. Learning tables was a nightmare; teachers wanting a quiet hour could set horrible sums of multiplication in any of the above measurements, or division, or subtraction. Even addition was usually beyond me. No wonder there was no hooliganism in those days, we were hard at it mastering all those beastly measurements.

We were more than halfway through the century before the yard and the pound were redefined in metric terms, and in 1965 the government announced that we would convert in easy stages to the metric system. There was then a great deal of opposition to this and still is by many folk; our counting systems had developed over many centuries and people resent changing their traditional ways. For instance, treasured cookery books of yesteryear make little sense to today's newlyweds; the measures of flour and butter have to be transformed from pounds to kilos. However, by 1978 most packaged products were labelled in metric units and in the 1980s we had to learn to measure our requirements for petrol in litres instead of gallons. Our coinage changed from the pounds/shillings/pence to just pounds and pence, and instead of 240 pence to the pound we only had 100, that happened in the 1970s. This process is nearing completion, as it must, because people under thirty have not even been taught the old measurements, and those under twenty do not comprehend inches and pounds.

Of course, now we have to include the "Euro", an odd measure of 'wealth' ordained by the European Community. So far it has not really affected us ordinary folk in Abbots Langley, but local companies, trading with partners in Europe, have to deal in euros.

In 2000 even in mainland Europe euro notes and coins are not yet in everyday use, but since the euro was introduced a year ago the pound has increased in value against it by about 13%. This helps us when we travel on holiday, but it is a problem for businesses, because any changes in the rate between ordering, invoicing and receiving payment can result in an unpredictable profit or loss. It is possible to insure for this, but the strong pound has caused some multi-national companies to re-think their manufacturing policy in this country, with some threat to employment.

The first Queen Elizabeth had decreed that one mile would be eight furlongs; now it is just under six trillionths of a light year – and that is totally beyond my imagination to comprehend even though furlongs had presented a mental block.

For the record, on one of the plinths in Trafalgar Square, London, is the precise measure for feet and pints, placed there by the Standards Department of the Board of Trade in 1876. Isn't it comforting to know that although we have to buy milk and beer in a shop in metric measure, in 2000 we can still have a pint of milk delivered to our doorstop and a pint of beer in our mug. And the Manor House cricket pitch will still be twenty-two yards long!

A Busy Weekend
September 4-5, 1999

Janet Palmer

It promised to be quite a busy weekend. On the Saturday morning I went into Watford to the Friends of Watford Coffee Morning. It was good to have a chat to interested people and hear their ideas for further avenues we might explore for improving the awareness of people in the Watford area with the museum. Back home for a spot of lunch.

Earlier the previous month we had heard, during a service at the Parish Church, that Keith, the curate (The Revd Dr Keith Straughan, to give him his full name) had been "surfing the internet" and had found that a small Russian *a capella* (i.e.

unaccompanied) choir was visiting England on a tour. He had invited them to perform at St Lawrence Church as the first of a series of events to celebrate the new millennium. Accommodation was needed for them and, since we had some spare beds, we had offered to put two of them up.

So on Saturday afternoon we went to collect our guests from the church. We were assigned two ladies, both called Irina, and took them home for a wash and brush-up before returning them to the church hall for a meal and a rehearsal. Neither of them was speaking any English and our Russian is non-existent. This was not going to be easy!

We attended the concert in the evening. The first half was religious music from the Russian Orthodox Church and the second half consisted of folk songs. I didn't know them at all – and I suspect neither did anyone else – until they burst into the Beatles "When I'm Sixty-Four" as an encore, but they held us spellbound. Such powerful, rich voices, were there really only six of them? A truly marvellous, moving experience.

We returned home with our two guests. Not yet bedtime, how were we going to entertain them? However, it transpired that one of them actually spoke quite a lot of English. She had visited the UK several times with choirs. For the other it was her first trip. All six were professional singers and a foreign tour earned them far more than in Russia. Over cheese, biscuits and wine we compared notes on ways of life, education, families, and tried to learn with little success the names of the months from a calendar which one of them had given us.

The next morning we took them up to the church a little early as they were taking part in the service. After an interlude back home with our two in the lovely sunshine in our garden, all six were being treated to lunch at the Viceroy of India restaurant. We decided to join them, as did some of the other hosts, and it was a delicious meal. It was now time to wave them off in the minibus on their way to Southend, for the next stage of their extensive tour.

Whether we shall keep in touch with our guests remains to be seen, but by being involved in this event we certainly felt, as newcomers to Abbots Langley, that we belonged a little more in this community, where we have met already so many friendly and welcoming people.

A Week in the Life of a Villager

Rosemary Burrows

I was born in Tunbridge Wells, Kent in 1934, one of five children of Wilfred Ellis, who lost his job when electricity wiped out the gas company in the village of Burwash, Sussex. My grandmother at that time worked for Lord and Lady Southwood, in Highgate, London. Lord Southwood was the head of Odhams in Watford, and he suggested my father should come to the area and try for a job. This resulted in the family moving to Abbots Langley in 1938. I went to Abbots Langley Church of England School from the age of four and a half, as Maureen, my friend, wouldn't go without me. I then eventually went to Langleybury as it opened for about half a term. I trained in a day nursery in Leggatts Way, Watford, and eventually worked as a private nanny in St Albans. After the children were teenagers I went to work at Rolls Royce as an Administrator until it closed, then worked at Mount Vernon and then Watford hospitals until retirement. I married Bob Burrows in 1955 and had two children, Christopher in 1957 followed by Stephen in 1959, and now have three granddaughters and one grandson.

This is a typical week in my life during July 1999, starting on Sunday when I visited one of my sisters who lives in Essex for the day.

On Monday it was my turn to man the Good Neighbours mobile telephone which consists of taking bookings from usually the elderly for lifts to hospitals, dentists, clinics etc.; we are very short of drivers, especially in holiday periods. In the evening I attended a meeting of "Abbots Langley Forum". The first topic was the proposed altering of Watford and Hemel Hempstead hospitals into clinic types with possible day surgery facilities, and building a new hospital for ordinary surgery with wards for longer stay patients. This was discussed at great length, the majority of people being against it. We have another six hundred-plus houses newly built on the Leavesden and Abbots Langley hospitals site and everyone felt we needed more medical facilities, not less. We then went on to discuss the Millennium Studio building plans, but there was really nothing to report other than that the new feeder road onto the A41 was complete.

The next morning, Tuesday, I went to Yvonne Morton's at Kings Langley to make more craft items and price up for her intended charity stall at Hemel Hempstead; this is for the Kings Langley Guides hut to be extended for storage purposes. In the evening we did our usual stint of helping with the 1st North Watford Scouts fundraising bingo.

On Wednesday I went to Watford General Hospital for physiotherapy on my shoulder – I broke my arm thirty-three months ago and it still isn't perfect, possibly never will be. It was the Women's Institute meeting in the afternoon and I am door keeper at the moment; we have about fifty members. Later I went with Bob to Tesco's at Jarmans Field, Hemel Hempstead to do the main shopping.

Thursday it was time to give the house a thorough clean instead of a quick flip, and I did three machine loads of clothes washing. In the evening we went to the Gardens of the Rose at Chiswell Green for a concert in aid of the children's charity HOPE; it was very enjoyable, with children doing Irish dancing, a steel band, and a choir.

On Thursday I went to Hemel Hempstead to see two of the grandchildren, Alex and Mark, and made an evening meal for a friend.

Finally on Saturday I went shopping in Watford in the morning, and then the other two grandchildren, Stephanie and Zoe, came to stay for the night.

Local Transport 2:
Travel by Train at the Millennium

Tony Manning

The Railway looking north-west from Gypsy Lane bridge, February 2000. Photo: Reg Nice

Travel by train is showing healthy growth as a result of a conscious effort on the part of Government and pressure groups such as the "Green" movement to persuade people to reduce their dependence on the motor car. It is perceived as environmentally friendly since most trains now rely on electric traction and are separated from pedestrians and other hazards running on their dedicated tracks. Accidents are widely reported as they are usually spectacular, but they are rare and train travel is perceived as safe, which statistically it is. Of course the electricity used has probably been produced by the combustion of natural gas, but this detail is lost in the environmental argument.

Kings Langley station, 1990. Photo: Eve Durtnall

Investment in the railways has been very fitful since World War II, the local line from Euston to the North West via Watford and Kings Langley having been electrified in 1968, with very little else of note until privatisation in 1995. In the years leading up to privatisation all investment by the State railway company ceased, with the result that the railway construction industry and rolling stock manufacturers largely went out of business due to lack of orders. Immediately after privatisation there were demands from customers and from government (which now had a different party in control) for substantial and immediate improvements. Investment has increased but the improvements are lagging. On the local line orders for new trains capable of running at 240 kph, against the present 170kph, have been placed for delivery in 2003, mostly manufactured in Italy, and there are plans to upgrade the track and signalling. Journey times to, say, Glasgow, could be reduced from five hours to three and a half, which is comparable to the overall time for air travel.

Plans for trains travelling direct to a variety of European destinations through the Channel Tunnel, and calling at Watford from the North, have been put on hold as a result of the success of low cost air travel. Since privatisation passenger traffic has increased by 25%, and there is both an increased frequency of trains and some interesting new routes, for example an hourly service from Watford to Gatwick Airport via Olympia. In fact traffic density is now at a level which is causing delays and may be impacting safety.

There has been some growth in freight traffic too, with trains marshalled at Wembley for journeys through the Channel Tunnel to distant European destinations.

Train travel is the one area of public transport that has had some success in wooing motorists from their cars, with successful new light railways in Manchester, Sheffield and Newcastle, with one under construction in Croydon, together with extensions to the London Underground system that have opened with great success recently. Locally we are already well served by the radial lines from London. The Metropolitan Railway and the St Marylebone/Aylesbury line passes through Rickmansworth, the North Western Main Line from Euston through Watford and Kings Langley and the Midland Mainline through St Albans, with the Great Northern a little further away at Hatfield. Not so easy is travelling from East to West. The service from Watford to Croxley ceased some years ago although the Watford/St Albans trains still run, but stop short of linking with St Albans City station, although the tracks pass within less than half a mile of each other. There is a firm proposal to link the Metropolitan Line at Croxley with the old line to Watford Junction, which would serve as the basis of a local railway system which would have a realistic chance of attracting new business from car drivers and their passengers.

Putting the Abbots Langley Local History Society Journal together

Audrey Ashby, Editor

It was after the inaugural meeting in May 1994 that the late Dennis Hubbard (the Society's first Chairman) asked me to be Editor of the Journal. Having always taken a keen interest in history and also having made a study of genealogy for many years, I was very happy to take up the challenge – one which has proved to be a most pleasant and satisfying venture.

Although I live in St Albans, my family originated from Abbots Langley so I have a strong affinity with the village. During World War II (1939–45) I lived at my grandmother Phillips' house in Trowley Bottom – now Tibbs Hill Road – and sometimes stayed with friends, the Bonsey family who lived in Abbots Road. For a while I went to the evacuee school near the church until I was five, which I remember very well and where my grandmother would clean and light the fires in the school.

Some years ago when researching my family history, I discovered that many of my earlier ancestors dating back to the 1700s had also lived and worked in Abbots Langley. They were christened and married at St Lawrence Church and some were later buried in the churchyard. I learnt that during the 1920s my grandfather Tomlinson had worked for the church as a gravedigger and that he too was later buried there, quite near where my father, uncle and grandparents are buried in their Phillips family grave.

From all this personal research I was able to build up a store of material which in turn enabled me to continue with further research on the village and its people for the Journal. I spend many hours in the Record Offices and Libraries seeking out those little "gems" of information about the many people who have lived in and around the area and who have played a vital role in the order of things. Some stayed only a short time and others lived in the village for many years – but all have left their mark and helped to make significant contributions to Abbots Langley and its evolution.

Apart from using my own material I receive a considerable number of most welcome articles, letters, poems and photographs from Society members near and far – all of which help to give the Journal its general appeal and is a vital ingredient to its success. Relatives and friends have an important input too, and I enjoy visiting them for a chat about times past. I often interview the local elderly residents and many of their stories appear in the Journal, especially in the "I Remember" spot, as they recall their school days, work or life in general. This often brings in the delightful letters which are fascinating and a joy to read, adding little anecdotes for inclusion, too.

I am pleased to say that the Journal has grown steadily over the past six years both in content and in sales. All of this is very encouraging and fortunately there is still plenty of on-going material to fill the twice-yearly issues – yet despite this there are certainly more untapped sources waiting to be unearthed.

The variety of history topics includes something for everyone – for those who want only a light read, with snippets of information on the past weather and folklore, to the more factual articles on the village and its people for the more discerning palate. There is a page for family history and another which records the Watford Observer reports on Abbots Langley one hundred years ago (thanks to its Editor). The centre pages usually contain the lead article which also has a marketing flyer for display in our sales outlets.

We sell the Journal throughout the monthly winter meetings, at the Abbots Langley Carnival in June, and at the local chemist shop. There is also a mailing facility for back copies, or those who wish to subscribe. Our out-of-area members receive a complimentary copy with their subscription, and complimentary copies are also sent to the British Library, local Libraries and Record Offices, which keep people aware of our existence. As I write we are now on the website (thanks to Robin Mann, production) so we have certainly come a long way since we started in 1994!

The front cover of the Journal shows either a local building or scene beautifully sketched by local artist Prue King. There is a "photo spot" from local photographer Eve Durtnall, and the back cover page is usually an old advertisement courtesy of the Watford Observer or the Parish Magazine. Many of our contributors are now "regulars" and they often send a photograph too – all of which helps to make the Journal a good read at 75 pence a copy.

After sorting, collating and typing the material for each twenty-page issue, I then hand the copy to Robin Mann who puts it all onto computer before the Journal is finally "put to bed" at the printers in May and November. Then it's time to start thinking about the next issue as I head off towards the Record Office once more ...

Being Journal Editor has given me endless opportunity to research and write about Abbots Langley and its past. It has also enabled me to meet, chat with or interview the villagers from all walks of life – for without people there would be no village! The research has also taught me too, for while it presents a wide canvas on a different world it can also help to put today's lifestyle into perspective. It is quite uncanny, when researching, to discover from history so many things which are similar to those we experience today! Perhaps it is true after all that "history repeats itself"? I wonder if those who read this in fifty or one hundred years' time will think the same. I wonder, too, if perhaps throughout the ages there is a fundamental sameness in people – despite how complex we often seem?

Whatever we discover about history there are many ways of reproducing the findings, whether it be writing, painting, photography or the new technology of computing and digitalisation. It is with this thought in mind that I hope the Journal of the Abbots Langley Local History Society will play a part in the grand order of things in the future.

For me personally, if history continues to be recorded by

whatever medium and there is access to it for future generations to learn from, then I am happy. As I write in March 2000 that is my wish for the Journal, and long may it continue.

A Day in my Life, May 1999

Revd Stephen Fulcher, Abbots Langley Methodist Church

My day usually begins about 7 am when I take my dog for a walk. Our first walk of the day is usually for about an hour. We set out from the Manse in Abbots Road and walk over the pig farm towards Bedmond if it is dry; this involves crossing the footbridges over the M25 motorway and traffic going west is usually very heavy and barely moving. There are many heavy lorries as well as cars – mostly with one occupant – on their way to work. The noise of the traffic is relatively small, because it is moving so slowly. On a wet day we are more likely to stay on made-up footpaths in the village, often exploring the new housing areas on the old Leavesden and Abbots Langley hospital sites. The village High Street is almost deserted at this time in the morning, and apart from the postman, newspaper delivery boys (they all seem to be boys) on their bicycles, and milk deliveries, there are also a few other regular dog walkers and we exchange a greeting and some light conversation.

On my return to the Manse I have breakfast and then shower, and begin the working day.

Work begins with a time of prayer and Bible reading. Often the telephone rings to interrupt, but I usually leave the answering machine to deal with early calls. I then sort the post and make as many replies as possible. Then there will be a number of telephone calls to make, answering the messages left, and catching up with events of the day before. Routine calls may include funeral directors, crematoriums, catching up with news of people in

Abbots Langley Methodist Church

hospital, arranging details of weddings and baptisms, and arranging agendas for church business meetings, and so on.

These letters and calls completed, I then assess the priorities for my day. Often an unexpected emergency such as a sudden death or a seriously ill person taken to hospital, can throw out all the day's plans. Fortunately there are no such situations today.

My responsibilities cover the Methodist churches in Abbots Langley, Kings Langley and Croxley Green; that is around two hundred and fifty people to care for in the church, and other community activities. At 11 am today it is my turn to take the Christian worship service at the Abbeyfield old people's home in Kings Langley. This service is led by leaders of all the Kings Langley churches in rotation, so I spend half an hour thinking about what I will say. Were I to be taking a school assembly or visiting one of the pre-school playgroups that are held in our church halls, this is the time that would happen. On a Friday morning, I usually prepare the content of the Sunday church worship.

I do not usually stop for lunch, so after the service at Abbeyfield

I visit an elderly lady who attends church usually, but has not been for some time because of ill health. We might take Holy Communion together, in her living room.

By 2 pm I am at Croxley Green Church to lead an afternoon Bible Study group of about fifteen people. This group meets every other week, comprising retired people and non-working parents who need to be away to collect their children from school by 3 pm. I might visit someone after this while I am in Croxley Green, and then go back to the Manse to take the dog for another walk. Today we walk along the Grand Union Canal, and during the walk I stop and talk to three people I know from church.

Back at the Manse, I feed the dog and then myself. There is then one hour to prepare for the evening activity and to answer the telephone calls that have been made during the day.

Tonight I am leading the Youth Group at Abbots Langley church, on the subject of "The Wisdom of Jesus". I plan a short talk, and games and activities related to this theme. Twelve teenagers gather from 7.30 to 9 pm to take part in the evening I have planned, and it is great fun. Often I would visit another family to discuss a baptism, wedding or funeral, or some personal problem, after the Youth Group.

Tonight there is no one awaiting an urgent visit so I return to the Manse, have supper, take another short walk with the dog, make a few more telephone calls and then spend half an hour reading a devotional book, a prayer, and then bed by midnight at the latest!

Who knows what tomorrow may bring?

I Remember

Pat Holmes

While reading that street parties may well form part of our local Millennium Celebrations, I recalled memories of "The Crescent" VE Street Party, a wonderful and friendly event.

*[Editor's note: VE Street Party – across the country street parties were organised to celebrate **V**ictory in **E**urope after the 1939-1945 War.]*

Then, we had no shortage of willing organisers, for the folk who came forward not only offered their time but, like every household in the Crescent, part of their precious food rations. Village shopkeepers also gave a helping hand, greatly appreciated.

Horse and cart rides provided by Mr Gray (in dark suit). Photo: 1945, Pat Holmes

Above: Street party, The Crescent. *Below:* Crescent helpers – two small girls on left hand side: unknown; left to right standing: Mrs Nightingale, Rose Lee (Mrs Baldry), Betty Wells, Mrs Joplin, Mrs Parmeter, Mrs Biggerstaff, Mrs Jess Bromley, Mrs Stafford, Mrs Brown, Mrs Winchester; left to right seated: Mrs Jones, Janet Heilling, Kath ?, Mrs W Hourahine, Mr Ben Bromley. Photos: 1945, Pat Holmes

From such an assortment of generous gifts other helpers prepared a successful table of treats for the children.

Adding to their amusement, Mr Gray provided rides on his horse and cart, and enthusiastic youngsters certainly kept man and horse busy.

Elderly Mr and Mrs Trendle, happy in knowing they could also contribute towards that day, agreed for their piano to be moved into the Crescent, where Mrs Lee played and everyone else gathered around for a merry sing-along.

Hopefully others will recall a friendly face from the band of helpers in the photographs.

Some of the Local Societies I belong to in 1999

Jane Lay

I have been a member of the Abbots Langley Local History Society since its beginning, and have enjoyed every social evening that I and my husband have attended. Although I was not brought up in Abbots Langley I have lived here longer than anywhere, so you could consider me to be a local by now.

The meetings bring to light the village and what it used to be, and when you walk through the streets you can visualise what it was like many years ago. What a shame it has been spoilt and so many houses have been built in and around, but we can always look and hear about our history thanks to the hard workers of our committee.

I have belonged to the Abbots Langley Social Liberal Democratic Party for nearly twenty years. Through working for the political party I had the honour of being one of the four people elected onto the Abbots Langley Parish Council in the 1987 elections. The

Cricket and the Manor House Pavilion, 1991. Photo: Eve Durtnall

committees I mainly stood on were the Playingfields and Leisure Committee, and the Footpaths and Allotments Committee. In my third year I was elected by my fellow Councillors to be the Vice Chairman of the Parish Council and subsequently became Chairman in the following year. In my year as Chairman the New English Wood was planted in the dell below the Manor House fields, and today the growth of the trees has been superb. These trees are the future wood for our grandchildren. In my year also I had the honour of representing the Parish Council at a Buckingham Palace Garden Party.

I also belong to the Abbots Langley and District Horticultural Society, and am proud to have been their Secretary since 1984. This Society is one of the oldest in the village, originally starting before 1866 and I believe is one of the oldest horticultural societies in the country. We run social evenings in the Manor House Sports and Social Centre, and have the annual horticultural Show in September, and have a shop in the Manor House Allotments where members can buy an assortment of gardening accessories. Our history is interesting because of the age of the society, and we can boast many familiar names that have been associated with it. In 1978 we organised the BBC radio programme Gardeners Questiontime to visit Abbots Langley when over 140 villagers attended, and in the following 1984 Clay Jones, the famous gardener, came to talk to over 200 villagers.

Another club I belong to is the Abbots Langley Cricket Club, which goes back before 1855 and they play on the Manor House Grounds in Gallows Hill Lane. I have been a member for over twenty five years, and at present hold the job as Membership Secretary. I have been making cricket teas for most of those years, and providing lunches for all-day matches for twenty years now. As well, I have been Assistant General Secretary, typing letters and reports and taking minutes, scorer for 1st, 2nd, 3rd and colts teams, and brought up two sons James and Matthew who play for the Club. My husband Leon who is an Honorary Life Member of the Club has been a playing member and umpire, and is still playing, for fifty years. We both support the Club wherever and whenever we can by working behind the bar, cleaning the clubhouse, running the colts and on the committee do anything else we can to help the smooth running of the club.

We have two allotments on the Kingsfield Allotment site behind the Compasses public house, where we grow assorted vegetables and fruit. We now grow lots of dahlias which we show in the horticultural show. Life can be very hectic, but peaceful on the allotments and everything depends on the weather. We are never satisfied; we need sunshine and heat to make things grow, but too much and the seeds do not germinate or the plants die. The constant watering when the weather is too dry is a real chore, and then when the rain starts it never seems to know when to stop.

We both belong to the Abbots Langley Bowls Club in Langley Road. Although we only play a couple of games a year, and maybe visit the clubhouse a few times, they are always so welcoming, and it is so peaceful to sit and watch the players rolling their woods up the green.

In all of the clubs I belong to I have made many friends and colleagues, and would not have missed my association with them for the world.

A Typical Day in the Life of a Local Councillor at the end of the 20th Century

Paul Goggins

At the end of 1999, I was the Hertfordshire County Councillor for Abbots Langley Division, and Three Rivers District Councillor for Langleybury Ward. The following account is not untypical of any day during the period from 1985, when I retired from full-time employment, to the end of the century.

- 7.30 am: Leave my home in Hunton Bridge for County Hall, Hertford. During the peak period in the school term, one would have to leave an hour to make this journey of just over twenty miles, but outside the morning and evening peak periods it would take just thirty minutes.

- 8.30 – 9.55 am: Receive comprehensive briefing in my office from several County officers in preparation for my chairing a meeting later in the week.

- 9.55 – 10.25 am: Clear mail from my pigeon hole at County Hall, dictating replies, telephoning, filing papers.

- 10.30 – 11.55 am: Attend principal Committee meeting in the Council Chamber, and making a contribution to the debate on a local issue.

- 12.00 – 12.30 pm: Drive home to Abbots Langley for a quick lunch.

- 1 – 2.30 pm: Attend meeting of the Abbots Langley Early Years Forum at the YMCA, Woodside. In the absence of the regular Chairman, I was asked to chair the meeting of social workers, educationalists, organisers or child minders, toddlers groups, etc. Modest financial grants to several local organisations were approved.

- 3 – 4.10 pm: Go straight on to a visit to Parmiter's School. There are eight schools in the Abbots Langley Division: three Secondary, five Primary, and one Special (for children with Serious Learning Difficulties); I make regular visits to each school.

- 4.20 – 5.45 pm: Clear as much deskwork at home as is possible before dinner. In addition to the letters delivered by the postman that morning, there were e-mail, answerphone and fax messages to deal with. Several of these would have been from local residents seeking the help of their local elected member.

- 6.30 pm: Leave for Stevenage to take part in a public consultation, due to begin at 7.30 pm, on proposals to reduce the number of Primary School places. Three County Councillors, one from each political group, form a listening panel in order to report back to their groups the views of local parents and other interested parties. As there were no Liberal Democrat members in the north of the county, I and my colleagues had to travel some distance to attend this particular series of consultations.

On this day I arrived home well after 11 pm – not in any way an unusual occurrence. Maybe it was unusual in that on this particular occasion I had travelled so far, but it could have been one of any number of local meetings, many of which end quite late.

For instance, it might have been a meeting of the Three Rivers District Council, the Three Rivers Music Society, the St Joan of Arc School's governing body, all in Rickmansworth; or maybe the Chess Education Forum which takes place anywhere in the Chess area, or one of the many meetings held in Abbots Langley. These might include: Abbots Langley Local Area Forum; Abbots Langley Regeneration Advisory Group; Abbots Langley Library Users' Panel; Abbots Langley Home & Road Safety Committee; Abbots Langley Citizens Advice Bureau Management Committee; Abbots Langley Performing Arts; Churches Together in Abbots Langley; Leavesden Transport Group; the governing body of St Catherine of Sienna School.

In addition to myself, in 1999 ten other District Councillors represent Abbots Langley, and there are fifteen Abbots Langley Parish Councillors, all incidentally Liberal Democrats. Most have daytime jobs and could not devote as much time as I could to council business, but they all contribute a great deal of their "spare time" to servicing the local community in a similar fashion.

Local Transport 3:
Air Travel at the Millennium

Tony Manning

Air travel for the ordinary citizen became a normal occurrence with the growth of the package holiday industry in the 1960s. The initial demand came from holiday makers disillusioned with the British climate and wanting "Blackpool-in-the-Sun (guaranteed)"! The development of larger aircraft put this dream within the price range of many.

With many more people employed in service functions business travel also grew rapidly, while holiday makers demanded more exotic destinations over longer distances.

Abbots Langley does not have a local commercial airport, and is served by the four main London airports, Heathrow, Gatwick, Stanstead and Luton.

One of the most difficult and time-consuming parts of a long air journey is getting to the airport, and home again on return. Car parking for the duration of a holiday at an airport is very expensive, and, except for short business trips, most people use alternatives. Trains from Watford Junction and St Albans City serve Gatwick. Several bus services such as Cambridge City serve all the airports, the buses diverting off the M25 at Hunton Bridge to pick up local passengers. Other alternatives are to have friends or family to drive you to the airport, and meet you, or to use the local taxi service

At this time the air transport industry is offering three broad types of flight. These are the full service business flight offering the minimum of stress and providing food and sustenance so that clients will arrive ready to work. Secondly, at about half the price, is a no-frills scheduled service with direct telephone booking or turn-up-and-board arrangements suitable for independent travellers and families, and third, the holiday flights, also relatively cheap as part of the package, where most of the passengers are travelling together and will be met at their destination. Abbots Langley residents make use of all three types, and contribute to the steady growth of air travel.

Abbots Langley Appreciated

Marion and Arthur Capon

Arthur and I do not live in Abbots Langley! Indeed, until we became friends with Clive and Simonne Clark it was just a place "near Watford" in Hertfordshire. As our friendship developed, so did our acquaintance with Abbots Langley and some of its residents.

We were to spend many summer afternoons walking through the village and surrounding countryside, into the Church and accompanying Clive on outings of research for his forthcoming book "Abbots Langley Then – 1760 to 1960".

It is an acquaintance that has led to a great deal of pleasure, not least the monthly gatherings of the History Society and the many interesting talks on an assortment of different subjects, but also some very fascinating reminiscences from local residents about times past that have been presented over the time since the society's inception.

Abbots Langley, we are very happy to know you!

A Day in my Life, 17 May 1999

Mike Quinton

It began as a normal day when the alarm went at 6.20 am. When I was working for Kodak Ltd in Harrow, I used to get up five minutes later. Now I am retired but slower. Kate is still teaching at St Helen's School in Northwood, hence the early start. Ever since a certain narrowboating holiday several years ago when it was my turn to be early morning tea boy, I have got up first.

Kate set off in her Vauxhall Corsa at 7.15 am as usual. We have been lucky with our paperboy this year, and during school term time he delivers the Daily Telegraph at around 7 am, so I was free to read the paper with my breakfast – but not for too long because this morning was an office morning and anyway the temperature in the dining room was only 16°C.

I inspected the rhododendrons down the garden – wonderful – and also the back fence, still intact but I wonder whether I have shut out the foxes and hedgehogs as well as the louts?

I prepared several questions to ask our contact at Lloyds Private Banking. My father had died in December 1998. Since I am his Executor and was his Receiver, appointed by the Court of Protection, I know to expect half of his estate, which will be the price of his house, which I had been able to sell soon after he went into a home. LPB seems a good organisation to actively manage this legacy, but I need to be kept informed as to details regarding money and share certificates handed to them to start the account. Obtaining probate will probably take a few more months but LPB advise that we should be ready to receive the money and make it work. The result of my telephone conversation with LPB was to ascertain the answers to several questions concerning our investments, and confirmation that a written account of dealings so far concluded will be forthcoming. Since some shares are not performing as well as had been expected, we will have to decide whether to hold on, to sell, or to invest further and this means keeping a close eye on the market with LPB's assistance.

I checked our e-mail, to learn that Kathy, my sister-in-law, who lives in Adelaide, South Australia, has confirmed dates in July when she and her daughter Gilly would like to stay at Woodcote House, Chipperfield. I e-mailed back that these were now booked and that her invitation to our daughter Jennifer's wedding must be on its way from Lyon in France, where she is organising things. Jen is due to marry Steve Pécasse on 24 July. They met while they were working at the Hilton Hotel in Brussels and they are now part of the team trying to get the new Hilton in Lyon ready for opening – which should have happened last month, but things have been delayed by a flood in the building.

At 7 am this morning a box of fourteen English invitations arrived from Jen; Kate had already prepared first class (26p) stamps for me to stick on the envelopes and post them. I made a list of names, using an EXCEL spreadsheet, so that we can tick off replies as they arrive.

I went to the post box at 2.15 pm, which left me little time to get to Ruislip Crematorium for Hugh Bastin's funeral at 2.45 pm. I arrived at 2.41 (phew!). Kate had given me a good route: M25 from Junction 19 to Junction 17, then follow ordinary roads from Maple Cross to Harefield by Coppermill Lane, then Breakspear Road to Ruislip. Although I had not met Nancy Bastin, née Boyson, since 1954 at my cousin Freda's wedding to Dennis Boyson, Nancy's brother, she knew all about me. I met Hugh when he was also working at Kodak in Harrow. We continued our acquaintance through the Kodak Wine Tasting Society, and it was at one of those meetings that he reminded me that we were related by marriage. In 1995 he lent me his photographs of that 1954 wedding, so that I could copy them. Nancy was the bridesmaid and I was there in the pictures aged thirteen.

Several other Kodak people were there, John and Mrs Foster, John Winter, John Bee, Tony Swinson and Philip Sumner from the Wine Tasting Society, but also Peter Denton, Alan Coates, Madan Badali and the chap with a full head of hair which is now white – Reg (or Peter?) – who all worked with Hugh. I shall miss Hugh telling me what relation we are to each other.

After the service we drove in our many separate cars 2.5 miles to "The Case is Altered" in Eastcote High Road. We sat outside, and the pub people lit a gas heater there; the sun was shining but it was parky because of the wind. Alan Coates bought me a non-alcoholic lager – not my usual tipple, but I needed to be able to drive home.

I think a few people may have been going back to the house but I didn't know where that was. I did have a long chat with Nancy. She was a policewoman in Cheshire before marrying Hugh and knew quite a bit about the Quinton and Riley families, Mow Cop etc. My uncle Joe married Marion Riley, and Freda was one of their daughters.

I left at 4.45 pm and got home the 13 miles via Northwood Hills, Rickmansworth and then the M25 to avoid the traffic around Watford in thirty minutes. Kate was home first, and we had a ham salad, finishing the "off the bone" ham I had bought in Waitrose last week.

Then it was time for the Annual General Meeting of the Abbots Langley Local History Society. Tony Manning had already twisted my arm and Eve Durtnall had also asked me whether I would like to be chairman. I became chairman. My fellow committee members are obviously all hard working, especially Reg Nice, the secretary, so it should work well. Reg had arranged for a raffle and a quiz, and they happened, but I had to do my first chairman's bit by cutting the "I Remember" spot because it was getting late – 10.15 pm after an 8 pm start!

That was quite a day!

Household Repairs in Abbots Langley

Reg Nice

This is a very wide-ranging subject, but as in most other communities there is a good selection of specialist firms, shops and individual tradesmen who work from home, who between them can repair or service most of the machinery and gadgets we have nowadays in our homes. The same can be said for repair and redecoration to our houses as well.

The easiest way to get any repair job done is to choose an appropriate specialist from the Yellow Pages telephone directory and contact them by phone. Many now have mobile telephones so they can be found even when away on a job, or an answerphone service for response later. Most people however know of a reliable person to carry out what they need, and the best of them being very much in demand it's frequently necessary to wait days or even weeks for them.

There are quite a number of builders and decorators in the village and adjacent areas, and while generally speaking the larger firms prefer to carry out complete installations, items like painting, plastering and roof repairs are often carried out by small or one-man operations. While most of these people are good craftsmen, one occasionally hears instances of bookings being made and then the tradesman failing to arrive, and also examples of poor and overpriced work.

The largest demand for repair work almost certainly concerns electrical appliances, followed by plumbing and joinery work. We have in the village at the moment two good shops which sell goods such as television sets, washing machines and other electrical appliances, and who also repair any of these items as well as carrying out repairs to house wiring systems, TV aerials, etc. Many villagers patronise these firms.

There are several plumbers, all of whom can fix leaking pipes, taps, etc. and alter or add to existing installations. An annual insurance premium of around £50 will cover prompt twenty-four hour attention to plumbing emergencies. Domestic heating systems however are these days quite complex, gas-powered in urban areas, and faults often require attention to gas and plumbing and electrical systems. Specialists firms are then needed and these can be found in nearby towns. Many householders also take out service contracts for regular maintenance to boilers and other gas appliances.

Costs vary widely, typically labour charges of a minimum of £20 per hour are made, plus a call-out charge from £30 to £50, and the cost of the parts supplied is usually the smallest part of the bill!

Many people carry out their own repairs, though increasingly electrical goods are becoming more difficult to fix and sadly it is often necessary to throw away goods because it is cheaper to buy new than to attempt to repair, or because spare parts are unobtainable.

Do-it-yourself repairers are well catered for by local merchants and the large supermarket-type supplies such as Wickes, Homebase, B & Q and so on, though I have had sometimes to shop more widely for specialist materials.

Until recently I had done almost all repairs in my home myself, but now advancing years and creaky joints have caused me to pay others to do some jobs – I do find that a bit of a blow to my pride!

I was an Evacuee in Abbots Langley in World War II

Clive Clark

[The following are extracts taken from the 46-page record Clive Clark wrote, entitled "The Evacuation of St Paul's School, 1939½-1945½" and which he dedicated to "all those who made my evacuation a happy one".]

Introduction

At the outbreak of the war, I was eight years old. My widowed Mother's circumstances were not such as allowed her to enjoy a home of her own, so we lived in a Hampstead boardinghouse. ... I found myself in the care of a young couple without children of their own ... I look back on these years as happy ones.

The Journey

[Clive Clark lived in Hampstead, his school was St Paul's School, and just before war was declared the town-bred pupils were being prepared for the possibility of evacuation to the country by their teacher, Mr Walker.]

... Mr Walker started a series of "Hygiene and Naturestudy" talks in the school. He talked for a short while about rabbits and other small animals, but mostly about various attractively-coloured berries. He said that many of these were to be found growing on hedges in some parts of the country, and warned us that they would give us all a bad illness if we ate them, despite the fact that they looked so appetising. There were too many names for me to remember them all, and I recollect deciding never to touch any of them. The name which remained clearest in my mind was "Deadly Nightshade" – and that sounded ominous enough to deter anyone from sampling it. ... The most unusual occurrence of all, however, and one which did make us begin to take notice of the news, was the arrival at the school of about fifty German-Jewish refugee boys. We could not take to them immediately, because they did not speak our language. They wore "funny clothes". It was not until they began to learn a little of our language, and we too had been shifted from our homes, that we began to understand them, and in some instances like them. ...

... One evening I brought Mother home a note from school, and the following morning I was told by her to tell Mr Walker "yes". At the time, I did not of course appreciate the significance of this message – either the heart-searching that lay behind it, or the heart-rending decision embodied in it.

... The Friday was cold and grey when I arrived at school [at half past six o'clock] with Mother just before the appointed time. She waited for a short while with some other mothers who were there, all trying to be brave. But in a short while she had to be off to work in the city, and so kissed me goodbye, told me to write to her as soon as I arrived somewhere, that she would visit me in a month's time, and then departed.

...By nine o'clock we had formed into a long 'crocodile' in the playground, our rucksacks on our backs, and some of us carrying suitcases as well. I suppose that altogether there were about a hundred and fifty of us, ranging from three to sixteen years of age ... down the hill to South Hampstead station. ... an electric train, our carriage soon a shambles of bodies and bags. The question of where we were going, still uppermost in our minds, was answered at last. Watford! I had never heard of it before ... the first impression that I recollect was that the place was disappointing ... we were led half-left out of the station, across a road, and into what I later learnt was the Watford Labour Club. Here we were each issued with a carrier-bag containing food, which we were told was to last until the following Monday.

...The bus we got on was a roofless double-decker, seldom before seen in the place at which we were finally to arrive [Abbots Langley] ... and I recollect that we had some fun bobbing down below the level of the backs of the seats, because of the overhanging trees along Horseshoe Lane ... at last we did get to the top of Tibb's Hill, turn left, and roll to a stop outside a redbrick and flint-stone building, the village school. The final stage in our journey commenced as we were led in our party of thirty or so by a member of the WVS to the road in which we were to be billetted. .... I recall that I could not decide whether the number on the slip of paper I was holding was 11 or 77 ... I solved the problem by remaining quiet when 11 was called and answering to 77 *[the home of Mr and Mrs Smith]*. ... In I went. I had arrived.

Settling in

... I was now invited to draw round the table and take food with the rest of them ... lunch being soon concluded ... I sat down to write my first letter home. ... The layout of the village was simple, consisting chiefly of the High Street and Gallows Hill Lane, the Abbots Road, and Breakspear Road. ... From almost any part of the High Street, one could reach open fields after three minutes walk in any direction. This was certainly a great novelty for me.

... I was walking along Langley Road towards the village on the following Sunday morning when suddenly all the sirens in the place started to wail,and the other people in the road started to run in the opposite direction from mine. A loud calling from behind me ... and there was my alarmed foster-mother calling for me to return home at once. ...I was told that the sirens meant that war had been declared.

...For the first time in my life I heard the words "gentry" and "elite". Such people in the village apparently lived down the Abbots Road. I was also warned that the two village policemen lived in Langley Road, and that if ever I disobeyed instructions and went down to the canal, I would be reported to them, or else sent away to the "school" at Watford.

...The day of Mother's first visit soon arrived. ... She has since told me that she found me obviously happy, and herself went away content that I was in good hands. ... It was on the occasion of her third or fourth visit that she told Mr Smith, in front of me, that she gave him full power to punish me as he thought fit, and whenever he considered that my misbehaviour had warranted it. ... It was during one of these weekend visits that Mother asked me where I would like to live if "anything" should happen to her. I plumped for staying where I was ... the end of the trial period at 77: I had settled in.

The School Settles In

... At the beginning of the week after our arrival, the whole school assembled at nine o'clock in the morning in the playground of the village school. ... The weather remained sunny – it was still only early September – the classes of our school were to undertake a series of morning excursions which were called "Nature Walks" ... round fields and lanes that surrounded the village .. The walks invariably lasted until mid-day ... we scattered for lunch. During the morning the village children had taken their lessons in their school building. In the afternoons we used the village school premises, and the local children had time off. ... we used to sing as we walked ... "South of the Border", "I'm going to hang out my washing on the Siegfried line" and "There'll always be an England" were sung repeatedly. ...We always carried our gas-masks with us, and we knew that we might have to dive under a hedge if we heard an aeroplane coming very low in our direction. ... One morning .. the school trotted en masse across the churchyard, and round to one side of the Vicarage, where we found the Fellowship Hut ... our school building for the next five and a half years... into it were crammed about ninety children, a full-size billard table, a small billiard table, some cupboards, a piano, five gangways, five teachers and their desks.

... There were frequent sporting encounters with the local boys and girls, and in this period we were all-conquering at most games. ... At the end of the first winter term ... tobogganning... whole classes trekked down to the fields that lie between Gallows Hill Lane and the Abbots Road.

... Miss Rowlands, mistress of the infants ... unaccountably died ... although I was never able to find the grave, I believe Miss Rowlands was buried in the churchyard..... Mr Simons was master of Class 1 at this time .. Joined the Air Force .. Mr Walker taking that class. Miss Williams in charge of Class 2. Class 3 was taken first by Mr Parsons, then by Miss Hurley, and afterwards by Miss Buckoke. ... Miss Buckoke appeared almost from nowhere, but proved to be the daughter of a local funeral undertaker ... with dark hair, and lively dark eyes.

... Another feature of the early period was the practice of filing into the village church whenever the sirens sounded the alert ... we were never allowed to move around the church on these occasions, so we were unlikely to learn even a little of its long history.

... By the end of the first period the early attitude of the local people had been established ... they remained suspicious, and resentful that we had invaded their village. ... Mr Walker's chief problem ... to maintain agreeable relations with the villagers, and if possible build up some personal prestige. I think he did all these things, because the school did settle in.

My Lost Horizon

... London had for a long time been suffering from very heavy air-raids ... the village itself was not entirely out of the danger area. We were only eighteen miles from the capital, one mile to the east of the main railway lines going north, and the Grand Union Canal. However, the village received bombs only when the enemy were being chased away from London and felt themselves obliged to jettison their loads ... three smallish bombs fell at the bottom of my road, and another dropped near to the local cricket club's cherished turf ... an unexploded landmine floated down between the railway lines and the village. Half the juniors in the village were in the vicinity when this was exploded by the military .... just after the roar we heard ripping noises in the leaves of the trees ... later I picked out of the ground a large piece of bomb-splinter about a half an inch thick and about nine inches long by three wide.

... There were months of nights during which we were allowed only half our normal sleep ... sometimes Mr Smith was out in the street "firewatching" ... we drank tea as weak as water for hours on end and the guns sounded like blastings in distant hill quarries.

... I paid my first visit to London, and home.... London had a raid on the Saturday night, and I was brought back to the village the following afternoon. But at last I had been home again, after three years, and had made contact with the old world.

... Out of school time ... changed into old clothes and was out and away to the woods at the back of the road ... or perhaps further afield to the woods around Bedmond, or Kings Langley. The Smiths were great walkers and took me with them on their Saturday and Sunday evening walks around, say, St Albans, Bricket Wood, or Leverstock Green. I had pointed out to me details of all sorts of plants and trees ... learnt something of the various habits of many small animals ... Later Mother sent my bicycle to me ... very soon I had become quite familiar with all the country within ten miles of the village.

... Exactly how long the war would last nobody knew ... all plans for the future, and indeed any changes in the pattern of life, had to be postponed until the end of the war.

The School Jogs Along

... A figure of some minor importance in the school at this time was a lady by the name of Mrs Farden ... at the school all day and every day and did repairs on the spot for those amongst us who had the misfortune to tear our clothes, either at school or outside.

... The village Communal Feeding Centre was started and functioned in the village hall. Two sittings were held every lunch hour and I think it was originally intended that meals should be provided only for those evacuees whose landladies were away from home during the day ... the long practice of selling weekly supplies of next week's meal tickets in school on a Friday morning had begun and continued till the very end of our stay in the village. I went there once for a meal to give the place a trial before reporting to the Smiths, and I never had any desire to go there again.

... I was promoted to Class 2 ...to reap the privileges and pleasures of the senior school ... Miss Tomlinson took over from

Ovaltine Dairy Farm, 1988. Photo: Eve Durtnall

Miss Williams ... allowed to take part in the school's horticultural effort. ... The school possessed about an acre of ground along one side of the school playing field, on which it grew whever food it felt certain it could dispose of ... part of the national "Dig for Victory" campaign which the government had inaugurated at the beginning of the war. Successes with ... potatoes, onions, shallots, peas and beans, turnips and parsnips, spring-greens, brussel sprouts, cabbage and celery. The majority of the produce was sold ... mostly at reduced rates to staff and pupils.... Hoeing ... double-digging and manuring; ... cleaned and counted the tools ... ambled back to school where we could take those heavy, pinching clogs off. ... If the weather was too bad ... the gardening class tackled some "theory of gardening" from a Ministry of Agriculture [actually, Ministry of Food] handbook, of which I still have a copy.

 ... The boys' handicraft centre situated in the Bedmond Infants' School, run by Mr O'Niel ... one started attending the centre at the age of eleven years and devoted two afternoons each week learning the essentials of carpentry. ... The school also conducted a shoe-

Langley House, also known as Breakspeare College, Breakspeare Clinic and St Saviour's College. Photo: 1988, Eve Durtnall

repair service for its pupils. Shoes were collected from pupils at school early on Friday mornings, taken up to the centre ... repaired that morning and handed back to the owner at lunchtime. ... The renovations were done at low prices ... I think materials were provided by the County Council. ... I was one of the unfortunates who had to walk to and from Bedmond as often as eight times a week ... in the winter I found this boring but in summer I enjoyed it

... A local ARP *[Air Raid Precautions]* group paying a few weekly visits to the school in an attempt to teach the top class some elementary First Aid. ... talks upon anatomy and physiology were unheard in the uproar ... immobilising each other with bandages.

... About this time a group of us .. had what may be justifiably called a narrow escape ... with my back to the Ovaltine Dairy Farm when from over the trees of Breakspeare College came a "doodlebug" twisting and turning, stalling and swooping its way towards us. Its engine had already stopped .... we stood breathless, spellbound as we watched the silent spectacle ... squirmed its way across the field .. And landed two miles away at Felden with a loud bang and a cloud of smoke.

The Villagers

... Country life was no longer a novelty for us. We had exhausted the transient joys of "scrumping", were no longer likely to go to the fields just to look at real cows, more local fruit was left to its rightful reapers, and local farmers ceased to think that it was our delight to try to put their cows off milk .... we had become rusticated.

... Miss O'Kel, Billetting Officer for the village, active member of the local WVS; Nurse Jaques, with thick-lensed spectacles, ruffling pupils' hair with disinfected steel knitting-needles presumably looking for parasites; Miss Mary B – conducted a funeral undertakers' business – always to be seen swaying somewhere around the village on an old-fashioned upright ladies' bicycle, a tomboy girl grown old; Mr Ginger, churchwarden of the parish, a keen bowls player; Mr Drake, came to inspect our gas-masks which we carried with us constantly; Mr S, one of the oldest established butchers in the village ... also had strong connections with the village cricket club; Mr Dobson, the barber, his three sons away in the armed forces for most of the war; Mr Wright, village electrician, whose wife was postmistress of the local Post Office ... situated in the other half of his shop; the brothers Vine, kept a small general stores a little way along the road from where I lived, both handicapped by the loss of use of a limb; Mr Pascoe, local schoolmaster and expert snooker player; Mr Tibbles, onetime landlord of the Bricklayers Arms; Mr Creasy, the baker; Mr Kitchingman, the partially-blind church organist.

... A huge claxon siren was erected on the village green, and nearby was built a public shelter, for the protection of those villagers caught outdoors at the commencement of an air-raid. The new siren was allowed to sound only three times, before the whole village cried out that it was too loud to be bearable, and the construction of the shelter was so belated that the villagers just

Mary Busby, who ran a funeral business. She died 1973 and is buried in St Lawrence churchyard. Photo from a negative supplied by Mrs Miller (date unknown).

ignored it and the doodlebugs, and it went unused to the end of the war.

End of an Innings

... Almost anyone who settled in the village sent their children to the evacuee school. Where the children were less than eight years old they served to increase the already disproportionate size of the school's infants section. ... a building behind the Wesleyan Chapel in the centre of the village, had been taken over the house the overflow of infants from the Guides' Hut.

... Where sport was concerned, *[some pupils had returned to London because they were unable to settle down, some had reached school leaving age]* our numbers had sunk so low that we were obliged to amalgamate with the Roman Catholic boys of St

Saviour's College in order to make up two teams that would permit a reasonably enjoyable game.

... Mr O'Niel brought into the classroom some of the informal atmosphere of the handicraft centre ... he was agitated with the whole class ... steadily increased by the continuous giggling of Betty Rhodes, who was standing behind him, pouring out the day's milk allowance into beakers. ... The pattern of school life continued unchanged throughout the period. We all called each other by our Christian names, and our teachers called us by them too. The school garden and handicraft centre still flourished, and, together with sport, still occupied most of the summer afternoons. Friday afternoons were often the occasion of some indoor team-game, carried out in the classroom, or as was later the case, some reading aloud from a novel such as Scott's "Ivanhoe".

... The invasion of Normandy had taken place in the June of 1944, the Allied advance was pressing on apace. The school garden was not dug over that winter, and the handicraft centre was soon to be closed. ... how much longer could the war possibly last? ...What were we going to do when the school was no longer in the village? ... The last Christmas which the school spent in the village was the occasion of its co-operation in the manufacture of several articles for sale, the proceeds of which were to go to some good cause, perhaps the "Save the Children Fund". ... It was quite surprising the number of things which we could produce, working full time, for about two weeks. As far as the village was concerned, this production of knick-knacks was the last thing that we did. VE Day was on May 8th 1945 but I seem to recall that the school had officially left the village the previous Whitsun. The whole of the school property that remained was packed up and sent away within a week. ... burning operations took place outside in the playground, several of us helped in the destruction and I personally felt rather sorry about the whole thing because I felt that I was helping to destroy the past before I knew what the future promised.

... *[Evacuees having left school or drifted back to London over the five years]* when the day for the journey home arrived, we met at the village bus-stop, travelled to Watford Junction, where we awaited the arrival of the special train. ... Four got on, out of 150!

* * *

To me it was a sorry ending to a story which, on the whole, had been a happy one, yet one of the decline of the school from pristine health. It was also a story which had lasted for more than half the time that I could remember.

A Day in the Life of the Vicar

Canon Brian Andrews

The Parish Church of St Lawrence, Abbots Langley and Bedmond

Today begins early. Irene (my wife) leaves for Rickmansworth and the school at which she is head teacher. My pattern is much the same at the beginning of each day: bath; breakfast; newspaper, partly for information and interest, partly to inform my prayers; domestic chores; the post. I pray in two ways: one is at set times in church; the other is continuously, though not always explicitly. God is part of everything I do. Sometimes I think specifically about him, sometimes I do not.

At 9.00 am the Parish Administrator and I discuss the pattern of the day: what needs doing, who needs to be contacted, post and e-mails.

9.30 am is Morning Prayer and meditation for half an hour. Today this is followed by a Eucharist. The second formal prayer time will be Evening Prayer at 5.15 pm. This is a daily rhythm, a focus on God, an offering on behalf of the parish.

Then fifty students from a Watford School visit as part of their religious studies syllabus. I talk to them about the difference

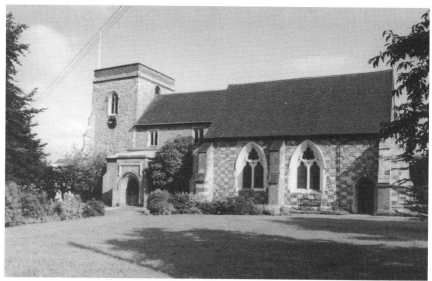

St Lawrence Church, 1992. Photo: Eve Durtnall

between churches and what a vicar does. They ask pertinent questions.

A visit to a family for whom I am to take a funeral. Then, after a snatched lunch, forty five minutes with a couple who have come to book their wedding. Funeral, wedding and baptism preparation takes time. Every one is personal and tailor made. There are no off-the-peg services.

This afternoon it is Tiny Tots and their mums in church. A story, a song, a prayer, and a noisy song stomping round the church with percussion instruments. Tea, squash, biscuits and, for me, paracetamol. Some afternoons are at meetings on diocesan or national church business. Some are visits to home or hospital. Some are sermons, articles, draft services, all of which have deadlines.

My energy level is at its lowest around 4.30 pm. If I'm out, I keep going. If I'm at home, I comfort-eat. Then Evening Prayer and time with my colleague (we also meet for an hour or so each Monday morning).

A bath – ideally every day because it refreshes me for the evening. Supper, which is usually microwaved. And then three hours of interviews, meetings or visits. Tonight it's a meeting at the Community Centre, tomorrow it will be planning the parish web site.

All through the day there may be phone calls. If I go to the shops, I am 'on duty'. People want to stop and talk, even briefly. On the one hand I am on duty all day, every day, and occasionally some of the night. On the other I have freedom often to choose what I do (or don't do) and when I do it. Hardly anyone will know if I'm idle or overworked, though if things don't get done, they'll notice. The workload is infinite. All most people see is the public face of the church, like services, but most of what a vicar does is less obvious. Life has four parts: church, community, family and me. They overlap. They often merge into one another. I have one day off a week and other times when a break from work is possible.

I'm so grateful that I don't have to commute between home and work. But I find it hard to relax at home because that is where work is. I work hard and I play hard. And I try to do both to the glory of God.

Millennium Eve Party

Peter Turner

This is an account of the Millennium Eve celebrations as experienced by an Abbots Langley family from the evening of December 31st 1999 to the early morning of January 1st 2000.

We, that is, myself, my wife Elsie and son Charles, had tickets for a party at the Headquarters of the Institution of Electrical Engineers (IEE) at Savoy Place in London. Central London was closed to all private vehicles and a number of nearby Underground

Stations were also shut, so we therefore paid more attention than usual to our travel arrangements. We left home around 5.45 pm, parked at Watford Junction Station and headed for Waterloo Underground Station. We reached there around 7 pm and crossed Waterloo Bridge to the IEE. Already there were many people about, all in a happy festive mood. The police were well in evidence, and mainly involved in assisting and directing. The absence of motor traffic made it possible to walk on roads usually jammed with vehicles.

The British Broadcasting Company (now Corporation) operated the world's first National Radio Station 2LO in 1923 from what is now the IEE Headquarters.

The building directly overlooks the Thames and we looked forward to our evening of music, dancing, a few drinks and the most important part, a good view of the celebrations. We were not disappointed. The balcony of the Riverside Dining Room afforded a wonderful view of the river. The Thames reflected the illuminated bridges and buildings, boats were ablaze with light, and in the night sky laser beams continually traversed. We could see the huge ferris wheel (the London Eye), Big Ben, the Houses of Parliament, St Paul's and many famous buildings and landmarks. We were to return to the memorable view many times during the evening. Below on the Victoria Embankment a vast mass of people continually circulated, flowing like the river. At the same time there was a cacophony of noise, singing, shouting, blowing whistles and general sounds of enjoyment.

At about 8.15 pm Concorde flew along the Thames at a very low height, with its familiar loud roar, unfortunately the even lower clouds hid Concorde from sight. At this time, fireworks and laser beams heralded the official opening of the London Eye – revolving so slowly as to make its rotation almost imperceptible.

The enjoyable evening passed all too quickly, and as midnight approached we gathered on the balcony to watch the face of Big Ben. As the chime of Big Ben struck, barges situated between the bridges burst into high-powered light, firing huge rockets into the sky, exploding into beautiful masses of stars and flames in

The London Eye, 2000. Photos: Peter Turner

patterns of gold, silver and many colours. The world's greatest fireworks display continued all down the river and lasted for fifteen minutes.

There were gun salutes from HMS *Belfast* and the bells of St Paul's rang out to welcome the New Year. Auld Lang Syne was sung, we toasted the New Year and continued to enjoy a few drinks. Our fellow guests, originally strangers, became wise and talkative friends.

The party finished at 2 am, and we made our way walking over broken champagne bottles across Waterloo Bridge to Waterloo Station. There were masses of people and the police advised us to go to Holborn Station. We retraced our steps and were similarly advised to walk to Russell Square, Tottenham Court Road, Goodge Street and finally and successfully to Warren Street Station. Thence we travelled to Euston and on to a welcome train to Watford Junction. We had walked about three miles, fortunately there was only a slight intermittent drizzle.

We arrived home at 5.30 am, and will remember and recall with pleasure our Millennium New Year.

A Day in my Life, October 1999

Geoffrey Flanders

On Wednesday 13 October – a fine dry day with lots of sunshine – I awoke at about 6.45 am to find my cat, Hawkins (an old family name) sitting on my chest demanding his breakfast.

I managed to pacify him until about 7 am, then got up and went downstairs to the kitchen where I fed him and laid the breakfast table. Then, having made tea, I took a cup up to my wife, Anne.

We washed, dressed and had our breakfast, consisting of cereal, toast and marmalade, and soon after 9 am I left the house and drove to St Lawrence churchyard. There, with my friend Brian Higgs and his son Nigel, we carried on with a project that has been occupying us once a week for some time, namely reducing by about a third in height an overgrown yew hedge in the Vicarage garden. The hedge had grown over the years until it was above the roofs of the bungalows in the adjacent St Lawrence Close, which used to be part of the Vicarage garden.

Brian and Nigel climbed up into the hedge, using a long aluminium ladder, and then proceeded to cut off the last six to eight feet of growth with hand saws and loppers. My job was to haul away the branches to the church car park, where the Parish Council workmen would either take them away on a small lorry or shred them on site, thus providing valuable mulch.

In the course of our work we discovered a path buried under soil at the back of the hedge, made from headstones dating from the end of the last century. We ceased work at 12.30 and I returned home for lunch, which consisted of cheese sandwiches and coffee, afterwards changing into more formal clothes for my afternoon appointment.

This was at 1.30 pm at the Hospice of St Francis in Berkhamsted, "An Induction Programme for Recent Volunteers". St Francis Hospice specializes in In-patient care for chronic illness, as well as a Day Hospice service for long term cancer care. Eight patients at a time attend one day a week for treatment, assessment, creative therapy, have lunch together, and enjoy social entertainment.

Volunteers could be nurses, cooks, gardeners, office workers etc., and drivers – which is what I have been doing since April. I either collect two or three patients from their homes at about 10 am and drive them to the Hospice Day Centre, arriving at 10.30 am, or I collect them at 3 pm from the Day Centre and return them to their homes. I find this work very rewarding, although I have to be prepared to lose them when they eventually succumb to their terminal illness. The lecture covered all aspects of the hospice functions, and was very interesting and informative. It concluded at 4.30 pm.

I then returned home to Abbots Langley at about 5 pm and had an early supper of pork chops, home grown potatoes and runner beans, and an apple crumble – with home grown apples, for dessert.

Leaving the house at 6.10 pm to drive to Harpenden, I arrived at the Public Hall at 6.30 in order to change into costume and be "made up" to appear on the stage with the chorus of the Harpenden Light Operatic Society, for their performance of Rogers & Hammersteins' "Carousel". This well-known and well-loved musical ran for six nights, from Monday to Saturday, with a matinée on Saturday afternoon. I have appeared in this musical twice before, in 1964 and 1984. The auditorium was about 80% full on this night, with full houses expected at the end of the week.

The curtain came down at 10.20, and I drove home to Abbots Langley, arriving at 10.45. I had a "nightcap" of hot chocolate and went to bed.

Another action-packed day in the life of a retired 65 year old!

The Grand Union Canal Now

Doreen Cooper

The Grand Union Canal has always been a favourite place of mine ever since I was a child in Hunton Bridge, and went to school in the original village school which stood at the side of this waterway.

In those days in the early 1930s there were still a few of the old broad horse-pulled barges, with boat families in traditional

Home Park Lock Cottage, February 2000. Photo: Reg Nice

Narrow boats passing the Ovaltine factory during a nostalgia run in the 1990s.
Photo: Doreen Cooper

costume, and the wives in full skirts and pleated bonnets. A peep into the tiny cabins showed their love of lace to edge the shelves, and the lace-edged china "ribbon plates" and gleaming brass. The same type of interior could be seen in the cabins of the "narrow boats" driven by engines which followed the horse barges. Both were gaily painted with panels of traditional "roses and castles" and every inch of woodwork painted in bright colours. The new narrow-boats no longer sported the tail of the previous horse on its steering tiller though. And canalside public houses no longer needed their stables for overnight barge horses.

As I write in 1998-99 very few narrow boats still carry cargo, although there is a society which aims to increase this cartage. The decline of cargo boats came in 1946-47 following the nationalisation of all transport by the British Transport Commission, under the Waterways Division which in the 1970s became British Waterways. A succession of hard winters when the canals froze caused business firms to change to road transport which they could rely on year round. The boats were all sold off or abandoned to rot, until a few enterprising people decided to copy the Norfolk Broads and use canal boats as holiday and pleasure craft. Now many old neglected canals are being restored by local enthusiasts who work hard to raise funds for projects like the "Wendover Arm" which leaked so badly and had been partly filled in. Gradually the old bright colours can be seen from the canal towpath walks again, and we can once more watch craft go through the old wooden lock gates using the heavy windlass winding gear.

End of an Era?

Ray Holmes

Around fifteen years ago, two local garages' forecourts provided a friendly and efficient service for one and all, greatly appreciated by motorists, who would readily exchange village banter with employer and employee alike. However, today, memories of such times rarely steal a mention in conversation. Understandable, of course, for our present wants are satisfied elsewhere. Yct even so, questions still linger about forgotten deeds, as for instance, 'who connived with who to obstruct the sale of petrol in Abbots Langley?' Late 1983 became the closure date for Flowers Brothers garage, although from a personal point of view it forms a datemark when Abbots Langley commenced to shed its village image, forever!

Motorists of the community reacted obligingly to their imposed plight, seeking out new refuelling places. A knock-on effect from this move was directed at shopping habits this time, and soon became crystal clear. Positioned around our parish outskirts – some completed and others still under construction – stood

FlowersGarage, which closed in 1983. Photo: Eve Durtnall

sizeable food store complexes. Each displayed a family household
name, such as Sainsbury, Asda, etc., and ample car parking
space, and adequate refuelling facilities for customer vehicles. As
intended, they proved to be an answer to a prayer for everyone,
none more so than respective store shareholders! Fully aware,
they now syphon off the life blood of local villages.

Prowling developers like hungry wolves sense distressful
situations. Therefore it sparked little surprise within village gossip
as planning permission allowed builders to erect accommodation
for elderly residents. One block of apartments was built on
Flowers garage was named "The Grange", and a second
construction known as "Hanover Gardens" stands at the village
entrance, Cecil Lodge end.

Sadly storm clouds gathered on the horizon when Leavesden
and Abbots Langley Hospitals, followed a little later by Rolls Royce
Aero engine factory, each closed down, bringing a terrible loss of
employment to the area, with other problems for the future. These
huge chunks of land stirred the imagination of planners and

developers alike, and a simple hint of things to come surfaced during a Three Rivers District Council public relations exercise around 1990. At a meeting held in the Parish Council offices in reply to a question on housing, a spokesman indicated that 900 houses would seem a reasonable allocation for the hospital site, while as to an allocation figure for houses on the airfield site, a positive figure is still awaited.

However, one certainty we can rest assured about is that eventually a sprawling mass of bricks and mortar will interlock Abbots Langley and Watford, as both Ganders Ash and Leavesden, faced with this setback, watch silently as their individuality disappears, wiped clean off many road maps now in print. In truth, our fate could differ little from our neighbours. Local historian and author, the late Clive Clark MA, concluded from research that "Langlai Abbatis" crept upon a map first dated 1086; who today would bravely suggest a date for our removal?

Unmistakably, a buzz of friendliness has departed from our village life. Left behind are people who appear as strangers to one another. Few recite a casual greeting, and nod with a gentle smile, truly the essence of village life.

Exactly how this Abbots Langley of ours will survive remains open for speculation. Perhaps a colourful Neasden-styled temple or a mosque would entice sightseers; we already have restaurants available, while our Manor House Sports field may appeal as an optional coach park.

On the other hand, this village may become the prototype for a dormitory geriatric annexe for the Watford Borough Council; a suitable probationary period reflects itself in today's village life. Over fifteen historical years not one councillor has accepted the gauntlet, to champion the cause of the village of Abbots Langley.

A Day in a Butcher's Life

Simon East

Good morning, everybody, it's Saturday at 4.45 am. It's time to get going, I jump out of bed and get dressed quickly as it's a bit nippy. I walk round to the other side of the bed and give my wife a peck on the cheek, and say "Bye love" and she replies as usual in an alien voice which sounds something like "Bye Bye" as she is still asleep.

Downstairs for a quick wash and shave, and brush of my teeth, a bowl of cornflakes and I'm off. The van is all icy, time to get scraping, and now I'm ready for the five-minute drive to Abbots Langley where my butcher's shop is. On my way I pass the Ovaltine factory, and the clock tells me the temperature and time: the clock reads 0 degrees and 5.20 am. There are not any cars on the road and only a couple of people walking their dogs.

When I arrive at my shop I park at the back and run round to the front door a bit quick as the wind is bitter cold. My first job is to put the kettle on for a cup of Rosy Lee. I put on my white coat and go into the fridge where I get all the meat and equipment I need to make sausages, put the mincer together, and mince the meat. I add cold water and seasoning to the mince meat and mix it up together, by this time my hands are freezing cold so I wrap them round my cup of Rosy and warm them while I drink, and then I finish off filling out and tying the sausages.

Next I put all the meat in the window: joints, chops, and everything else. At 8 am Adrian and Nathan arrive, they are my two Saturday workers. These days I can only afford Saturday staff, and business is not what it was several years ago due to supermarkets taking the lion's share of the trade. We put the price tickets out and get ready to open.

Then the postman arrives with all the bills – he once worked here as a teenager on Saturdays, and as he leaves he jokes "I'll be finished soon", knowing I will not be finished until 6 o'clock!

Simon East (centre) and Bob Roden, 1988. Photo: Eve Durtnall

Customers generally start arriving at about 8.30 am, and I chat and have a bit of a laugh with most of them; I often juggle with and throw their meat in the air whilst serving them. I have terms of endearment I use such as princess, sweetheart, blossom and my little pigeon. It puts a smile on their faces – I am told I have the gift of the gab!

The shop is empty for a while, then an attractive young mother enters the shop and I notice that Nathan and Adrian both quickly ask if they can help. Nathan by a whisker just manages to get his hand into the bag first. The lady required one pound of braising steak, and as he was weighing the meat his eyes were more focused on the lady who was bending down to see to her young child. As she stood up he said "that will be £9.80" and the lady replied in horror "How much? I only wanted one pound". Nathan's cheeks coloured – knowing full well that his eyes had not been where they should have been. Adrian and I nudged each other, smiling.

Lunchtime arrives and we buy rolls from the bakers next door and fill them with either my own home cured bacon or homemade sausages, which we cook at the back of the shop on an electric griddle. A lovely smell wafts through the shop and people come in and say "I feel hungry, are there any rolls to spare"?

During the day I have many orders over the telephone to deliver from people that cannot get out, which either Nathan or Adrian deliver.

Brian Andrews, the local Vicar for the past twenty years, walks past and I call out to him "Afternoon Grandad" as his son James (known to us as Jimmy the Vic) – another past employee and turkey plucker – has just become a dad.

Later two of my friends come into the shop: Ian Isaac the local GP, to arrange a game of squash, and Pete Alexander to arrange anything from a 15 mile cycle ride to an evening out, visiting just as many pubs!

Adrian has popped over to the bookmakers for a bet, and Nathan's on the phone to his girlfriend for the tenth time today.

Over the past twenty years that I've been open I have had many young people work here and a Saturday is the day that they will pop in to visit if they are passing by. We reminisce about times gone by.

Time rolls on and at about 4.30 we take the tickets out of the window, pack the meat away into the fridge – luckily not too much. We continue to serve the latecomers, and just as we finish and everything is washed, the chef from one of the local restaurants comes in and wants twelve pounds of mince. I put the mincer back together again, cut up the twelve pounds of shin, mince it, hand it to him with a smile, and as he leaves the shop I turn to the lads and say "B........ nuisance. Where's he been all day?" Oh well, it's all in a day's work. Without my customers I wouldn't be here.

As I leave the shop at 6.15 pm I make a mental note of what I need to order for Monday morning. There is no need for me to travel to Smithfield meat market or the local wholesalers, as all my ordering is done over the telephone and delivered direct from the abattoirs and wholesalers.

As we are entering a new millennium by law all meat will need to be weighed and sold in kilograms. However, up until now I have only been asked by one person for this measurement of weight – to which I am not disappointed!

Community Nursing in Abbots Langley at the end of the 20th Century

Wendy Beaumont

As we reach the end of the twentieth century, health care is a fundamental part of our civilised society.

There have been many developments in medicine and surgery over the past one hundred years, and our National Health Service is the envy of countries across the world (even though we may be critical of it ourselves).

As demands on the NHS have increased and peoples' expectations of treatments have grown, so the pressure on our local hospitals has become acute. The time spent in hospital has lessened and people need more care at home, in the community. This, together with the rise in numbers of very elderly people needing support and help, has had a significant impact on the Community Nursing Services. In Abbots Langley there is a dedicated team of nurses, led by a qualified District Nurse, working closely with nursing colleagues from the General Practitioner practice and from the Hospice at Berkhamsted to provide skilled nursing care to people in the community. They also work in partnership with Social Services to provide support and care to people of all ages with longer term disabling illnesses. The District Nurse is also able to access specialist equipment to enable her team to provide expert nursing care and, when appropriate, to link people to the overnight nursing service.

Alongside the District Nurses, within the Community Nursing team, are Health Visitors. In Abbots Langley there are two Health Visitors, and while they work with people of all age groups to promote good health, much of their time is spent with families with young children. In particular, new mothers find their support a lifeline during that first very demanding year of parenthood. By providing information on how to promote a healthy lifestyle and manage the various challenges of bringing up children, the Health Visitors hope to influence the health of future generations. They work closely with School Nursing colleagues who in partnership with local schools aim to continue the healthy living theme through the school years.

As in the past century, we can be sure that the next will see many more developments in health care and this, together with the increasing longevity of the population, will mean that the demands on our Community Nursing Services will increase. Some would also say that we, as individuals and families, will need to take more responsibility for our own health and health care. It is hoped that the plans for NHS Direct, a telephone help line manned by nurses, will enable us to do this more effectively.

A Day in my Life, May 1999

Maureen Denton

I awoke at 6 am on Sunday 16 May to see the bright spring sunshine filtering through the curtains of my bedroom. After opening the curtains I jumped back into bed to have an early cup of coffee and watch the blue tits feeding on the young red oak leaves on the tree that was planted thirty-two years ago when we moved into our brand new house in Dellmeadow. "O Eclesia" by Hildegard of Bingen was being played on the radio, and a large jet aircraft – maybe flying in from America – moved silently by in the sky waiting to land at London Heathrow Airport twenty miles to the south. "On Your Farm" was the programme on the Radio 4 wavelength and I listened to it before I began my Sunday morning ritual. Interestingly the farmer was talking about the Chillingham herd of cattle in north east England. These animals live as a herd roaming a large penned area of land as they did in mediaeval times, taken care of by a herdsman who cannot approach them as they are wild.

Peter, my husband, and I prepared to go to the Family Eucharist service at the Parish Church of St Lawrence at 9.30 am. About one hundred and fifty communicants were in the congregation; many come from the new housing area built on the old Leavesden Hospital site and those of us who have lived in Abbots Langley for a while are challenged to welcome them and to make them feel at home in our church. It was the Sunday after Ascension Day, and the message was endorsed "that we go out and spread the message of Jesus Christ" however difficult it may be for us, showing love and kindness to others. After the service we gathered in the church hall for coffee and the noise of us all chatting was deafening. That time, over a cup of coffee, is when business is conducted with friends that we will not meet up with during the coming week. A large number of the congregation work in the community as district and parish councillors, charity workers, Good Neighbours, on a voluntary basis. Our Parish Church secretary is at the hub of arranging rotas for transport, visiting et cetera and liaising with us all during the coming week.

This Sunday saw the end of the 1999 Christian Aid Week in the village; house to house collections had been made, and the week ended with a Simple Lunch held in the Methodist church hall at 12.30. There was no time to do anything of great significance before we walked up Abbots Road to the lunch, and we sat at a table with Roman Catholics, Methodists and their minister, Steve Fulcher, and other Anglicans, a good ecumenical mix. Why do

Christians still give themselves labels? All of us were friends who had worshipped in slightly differing ways. The lunch ended with a talk, a quiz, and a video which had given us the up-to-date facts on the poverty of a large part of our world. Hopefully some of these facts remained in our minds as we left to go to our comfortable homes.

Sunday afternoon was a time for us to spend gardening. We planted the remaining young plants that had been left in the cold frame whilst we were visiting our daughter in Yorkshire the previous week, and then mowed the lawns which had grown tremendously while we were away. The sun shone, and it was great to move silently round our small garden making sure the plants were not too overgrown by weeds.

I was cook for the evening meal, and as always if I have cooked, my husband cleared the table and washed up. Sunday evening was a good time to telephone our family. We have three married children: the oldest lives in Wales and is about to move house; our second son has just started his own practice in Stockholm, and our daughter in Yorkshire has just given birth to a baby boy, so British Telecom make a fortune out of our family telephone calls – therefore it was sensible to phone them in a cheap phone period!

At 9.30 pm we caught up with the world news in the great pile of Sunday newspapers and watched a little television before going to bed. I thought over the events of the day, and thanked God for all he has given to us as a family: warmth, food, shelter and the love of our friends and family – unlike the refugees in the Third World.

Local Transport 4: The Grand Union Canal at the Millennium

Tony Manning

The History of the Grand Union Canal

The canal was built, as the Grand Junction, just over two hundred years ago, towards the end of the canal era. Its purpose was to provide an easier high capacity link for trade between the port, the large local market and financial institutions of London, and the heavy industry of Birmingham and the Black Country. The earlier route had been via the Thames to Oxford and thence Brindley's narrow canal, but there were problems with the river and the overcrowding at those canal locks which were capable of passing only one seven-foot beam narrow boat at a time. In contrast the Grand Junction had fourteen-foot gauge locks for pairs of boats and was engineered to a higher standard, with barges and lighters from the docks utilising the four foot navigational depth as far north as Berkhamsted.

Modernisation

A programme of modernisation took place, largely as a job creation scheme, during the depression of the 1930s, when the name was changed to Grand Union following mergers with other Midland canals. Cargo carrying by pairs of narrow boats lasted longer on the Grand Union than most other canals, but by the early 1970s the improvements in motor lorries, together with the provision of purpose-built roads and motorways for them to run on, finally saw the last loads carried – coal from the Leicestershire mines to John Dickinson's mill at Croxley and West Indian lime juice from the London Docks to Rose's wharf at Hemel Hempstead, now a D.I.Y. store.

Parish boundary: the canal and old footbridge, Home Park, February 2000. Photo: Reg Nice

Unlike some other canals which had been disused for many years, the long term future of the Grand Union was never threatened since by this time the enthusiasts of the Inland Waterways Association, and others, had won the battle of minds in public opinion and obtained consensus agreement that canals should be retained for amenity use. Today, in 1999, the canal carries as many craft in the course of a year as it did in its heyday, but the purpose, and the problems created, are different.

The Boats

These may be privately owned or hired to once-a-year boaters, or floating hotels professionally crewed or they may be run by voluntary community groups. In this way youth, handicapped, elderly folk and others can get out and enjoy the recreational possibilities presented by water, countryside, the activity of working the locks and the pleasure of slaking the consequent thirst at a waterside hostelry. The boats mostly have all the

Hunton Bridge PJK 1892

comforts of a country cottage, that is with heating, cooking and shower facilities and comfortable bunks. They still bear a striking visual resemblance to the original working boats, and indeed some of them are conversions, being made of steel to withstand frequent contact with the brick and concrete lock sides, and having hull shapes to minimise wash at the slow permitted speeds.

Other Activities

While many people are able to enjoy boating, considerably more take part in coarse fishing and walking, hiking or cycling along the towpath, or simply strolling with the dog and enjoying the natural beauty associated with the water and wildlife. In places the towing path has been widened and levelled, using natural gravels for paving, so as to make it easier for walking and for wheelchair access. The canal itself, the flooded gravel pits and the canal reservoirs at Wilstone, near Tring, all support a rich variety of wildlife. Imported predators such as mink, released from fur farms by misguided "animal rights"' activists, have caused havoc among some native species, such as water voles and moorhens.

Ownership, Development and Maintenance

The canal, in common with most English canals, is owned by the State and operated by British Waterways, a Government agency. Finance comes from charges to the users, particularly boaters, the sale of the use of water to local industry for cooling or processing, and a government grant to maintain this public amenity. The engineering problems differ from the days of commercial use. The locks have been made lighter to operate, initially by the use of non-traditional hydraulic gear, but more recently a conventional ratchet gear and iron pawl is used. However using modern materials reduces friction and a protective cover is installed to prevent fingers being trapped in the mechanism.

Water Supply

Water supply has always been a problem since each boat ascending or descending takes fifty thousand gallons from the summit to fill the locks. Originally this was minimised by the use of "side ponds" which retained about sixty percent of the water, but their operation was not easily understood by novice crews out on a once-a-year basis, and maintenance costs, increased by inadvertent misuse, was high. Today's boating takes place mainly in the late summer, the driest season, which aggravates the problem. The solution has been to use remote controlled electric pumps to return lockage water to the summit, so that restrictions on the hours of operation or even complete closures of the canal are hopefully a thing of the past. There has even been a serious suggestion that the pumps should be operated continuously during dry summers to transfer serious quantities of water for the public water supply in the South East from the wetter North West, although it has been pointed out that the more acidic water could seriously change the ecology of the Southern canals, which is one of their chief attractions.

The future

English canals are now a recognised part of our heritage, and some long-abandoned stretches are actually being restored to full use. Given this background and its central importance to the national network of over two thousand miles of connected waterways, the future of the Grand Union seems assured. There is always a powerful public voice trying to ensure that the waterside remains in as natural a state as possible and that any developments should be sympathetic to the appearance and tradition of the canal, and that repairs and maintenance are carried out in as sympathetic a manner as is practical.

My Life in Abbots Langley in 1999

Elizabeth Manning

As well as completely re-arranging the house after a busy Christmas week with a five-day family party, a very important job in January was to open the 1999 filofax diary kept by the telephone and to enter upcoming events for Tony and me. That always brings us up with a start, how can we fit it all in – and I thought that once I retired (nearly four years ago) I might become bored! I had saved a lot of hobbies and interests to pursue vigorously when I gave up full-time work in London, and there are all those lovely books to read, places to visit, family history research to accomplish ... the reality is not like that at all.

Once all the regular and routine meetings for church and other voluntary groups have been entered, we make plans for family birthdays and outings, and interesting cruises on our canal boat, and holidays abroad, and tennis and golf days, and home fixtures for the Watford Football Club. Then I firmly score out one day per week for US to do something (or not do anything!) together. Of course, by the end of the second month of the year even these days have usually been filled in too.

We enjoy our involvement as members of the Abbots Langley Methodist church, and before the end of the year I find I have been "called" (or was it conned) into editing the church bi-monthly magazine for the second time. Then the small but enthusiastic Bible Study group which meets at our home every month also encourages me to read and research more – which gives me pleasure as well as exercises my brain. On a more practical note, throughout the year we both make preserves and marmalades for our stall at the church Rainbow Fair in November, and welcome the anonymous plastic bags of empty jam jars often left on our front porch.

As well as making little crochet items for our canal boat using the traditional canal patterns, I have made a collection of cushions for the boat in traditional canal boat colours using new techniques learned at the monthly meetings of Hemel Hempstead Quilters. I admit that I have several UFOs – that is, unfinished objects – which I cannot think what to do with, but I cannot throw them out because they are sure to come in handy for something. One item which is nearing completion as a result of HHQ is a bedspread for an eight year old grandson who has a fixation for dinosaurs; his cousin supplied the outlines for real dinosaurs, complete with their official names; another cousin placed the appliqué cut-outs on the background material in the chosen colours to match grandson's bedroom; it remained for me to put it all together. It has a special hidden pocket in which to keep pyjamas and bedtime storybook, and the whole thing is reversible – and sewn completely by hand. I can hardly believe I undertook such a thing – but that's what OAPs and grandmas do, isn't it?

When I was commuting daily to Grosvenor Square, London W1, I read copiously. Library books, paperbacks, real classics, anything and everything, and even did the small crossword in the Telegraph between Stanmore and Wembley Park stations. Six months into retirement I found I was paying hefty library fines; how could I not find time to read any more!

Abbeyfield Abbots Langley Society management committee meetings only come round every two months, but there is a lot happening in between times and as Public Relations officer I was involved in the annual quiz, plans for the official opening of the extension to the home, and a quarterly publicity leaflet, as well as keeping the media informed. Abbeyfield is a national charity providing very sheltered accommodation for older people, and the society in Abbots Langley is over twenty years old now. The committee are a group of dedicated local folk who have worked hard to keep the society moving forward as rules and regulations and requirements change.

Our canal boat is moored on the Grand Union Canal at the Dunstable and District Boat Club at Cheddington. Tony's involvement as Secretary means that every month we enjoy the members' meeting as well as a number of other social events and it is good to meet with other canal enthusiasts. He also organises their annual outing to somewhere special, like the Thames Barrier, Tower Bridge "insides", a trip on the "Waverley" (the last sea-going paddlesteamer) down the Thames to Whitstable. Sometimes there are spare seats on the coach and we can invite Abbots Langley friends from the History Society to join the party too.

We have a garden which we never quite got under control while we were working. It's about a third of an acre, all on the level thank goodness, but with a sizeable vegetable and fruit garden behind the pretty bit. Neighbouring cats visit our own cat to sunbathe; there are field mice, sometimes a hedgehog, and lots of pigeons and magpies, bluetits, the occasional blue jay, and once a green woodpecker. It is home to two families of foxes who do not intrude or do damage to our plot, and about fifty grey squirrels who lodge in the two larch trees. I recall a small catastrophe in March when the new gas fire in our lounge was not drawing properly. Investigation by the Corgi/chimney sweep dislodged a squirrel's nest with three very young babies in it. We will draw a veil over the end of that story – suffice it to say that the Corgi man was unable to handle the babies so it was down to me – and we now have a squirrel-proof cowl on that chimney. With all the trees around our home why on earth did they choose to nest in our chimney?

We love music and go to concerts whenever we can fit them in, privately arranged evenings in The Barn, the Abbots Langley Gilbert & Sullivan Society at the Watford Palace Theatre, and the St Alban's Bach Choir in the St Alban's Abbey Church are always included in our diary, as are the productions by the Abbots Langley Players – excellently acted and greatly enjoyed by all who attend. We always meet Abbots Langley friends at these events.

Earlier in the year I underwent major surgery at a hospital in London which while not in any way sinister did mean that I slowed down somewhat throughout the summer, and did a bit of delegating. Nonetheless, we still managed to host two Garden Parties for the Methodist church, both of which meant some fast tidying up and titivation in the garden, and thankfully the weather was fine and warm on both occasions.

I accompany Tony on some of his Institute of Physics Retired Members' outings, and in May went to Stockwood Park, Luton. In the outbuildings of this beautiful park and gardens I discovered a craft corner, and a young man who was making and repairing items made of stained glass. Well, when I was clearing my grandparents' home in North London a few years ago, I retained the 1860s lantern found in the attics which had been damaged in World War II, just in case I could ever find someone to bring it back to its former glory. This gentleman agreed to look at it and in fact made it as new, to my great delight. It now stands on their grand piano in our drawing room, with a battery-operated "candle" inside which reflects the beautiful colours of the glass. It's good to know that real craftsmen can still be found not too far away.

Our son and his family live in Watford so we see them frequently – Watford Football Club helps – and then our youngest daughter and her family have settled in Bletchley which is only less than an hour away so we can watch progress as they reinvent their house and we welcome their assistance as we struggle with our PC and the internet. We always take a day or two each month to drive to Castle Cary, Somerset, to visit our oldest daughter and her family and keep her up-to-date with Abbots Langley news – she went to the old junior school on the site of which was built the new library, and then to Langleybury. We enjoy train journeys and have taken the Midland Mainline Special to Chatsworth House and Hardwick House in Derbyshire – we do notice how it always seems warmer in Somerset, and it was certainly much colder in Derbyshire, than in Abbots Langley. The families keep in touch by fax as well as telephone, and our fax machine and the computer complement the reference books I have collected over the years when grandchildren telephone for help with homework!

We take slides and photographs as we travel, and are always pleased to give slide talks to church and other groups to share with them our travel experiences both in this country and abroad. In 1999 we had the opportunity to visit Ecuador, camping in the Amazon rainforest, and later to cruise on the rivers Rhine and Neckar in Switzerland and Germany, as well as to spend a couple of lovely sunny weeks in the Fenlands of England on our boat.

I am closely involved with my own family history society as chairman and editor of the bi-annual bulletin, and head off to the west country for the annual reunion of the extended family who come from across the globe – none from Abbots Langley, although I do get the bulletin printed locally!

This year a new venture was started, a book club. This small group of friends meets once a month, and twelve of us all read the same book within that month to discuss, debate, dislike or even dissent in a very friendly fashion over tea and biscuits. The books have been suggested by the local librarian who supplies sufficient copies for us all to borrow, and it is a very good discipline for us as we try new authors and make notes – or crib from the internet!

Abbots Langley folk in our experience are certainly not insular. Generally we find our friends are much involved in local activities, while at the same time have wider interests which take them into other communities and even other countries. In 1958 we were welcomed to the newly built Follett Drive with our baby daughter, soon to be joined by two more babies born at home with the help of the local midwives and health visitors. The new neighbours all soon got to know each other through the babies, as we became involved in local clubs, organised our own sewing circle, did our stint as babysitters. It's good that today Abbots Langley is not stagnating, we are not a closed village, and while newcomers are welcomed as we were Abbots Langley will continue to thrive as a real community.

Abbots Langley Art Club

Prue King

The Abbots Langley Art Club has been in existence for over thirty years. Kingsley Cannon was one of the founder members and he was President until 1976 when the well-known Watford artist, Robert Hill, took over. Annual exhibitions were held in the Watford Library and many familiar names exhibited including Brian Pleasance, Anthony Wildig, Gail Gibbins, Una Ridley and Marion Flint.

The following notes were extracted from some of the programmes from 1971 to the present day.

On Saturday 4 December 1971 the Art Club exhibited fifty-eight paintings, some being offered for sale at reasonable prices ranging from £2.50 to £25. Kingsley Cannon was President; G R W Blinkhorn, Chairman; A M Berry, Treasurer; Miss G Tompkins, Mrs Una Ridley, Mrs M Wood were committee members. The annual subscription was £1, or 50 pence for Old Age Pensioners and students.

At the 1972 Show, sixty-eight pictures were exhibited and the display was extended to include some period costumes and dolls, and seed collages.

Eighty-three exhibits were displayed in the Methodist Hall and proceeds were dedicated to the 1973 Christian Aid Week. By 1974

Art Club Exhibition, High Street, 1990. Photo: Eve Durtnall

two exhibitions were held, in May for Christian Aid Week again, and in June to boost the Club's funds.

Interest continued to grow and members' work was regularly exhibited at the Watford Library as well as in Abbots Langley and by 1977 the annual programme included monthly activities such as slide talks, demonstrations and visits. The members continued to meet each Monday evening to work their own paintings.

By 1978 Robert Hill had become President and the Chairman was Anthony Wildig; the subscription was increased in 1980 to £2 per person. However, by 1982 costs had increased and full subscription was £3, £1.50 for OAPs and students, and for the first time a raffle was to be held occasionally for the club's funds.

It was recorded that in 1981 at one of the exhibitions a painting had been stolen. In 1983 the first of the Open Air Exhibitions was held outside Causeway House as well as an exhibition in the Watford Library and an Art and Craft Sale in the Henderson Hall in the autumn.

In 1984 Gail Gibbins became Chairman, Una Ridley was

Treasurer, and the Programme Organisers were Lynda Sutherland and Prue King; the three committee members were Anthony Wildig, Marion Hawkes and Jessie Holt. They were joined in 1985 by Mary Seabrook, Elsie Horn and Christine Hings. Slide lectures, demonstrations and exhibitions were included in the Programme as well as the regular weekly meetings.

From 1985 until 1989 Marion Palmer (née Harkes) and Prue King were Programme Organisers and during this period there were regular criticism evenings with Robert Hill as well as talks and demonstrations on subjects as varied as calligraphy and problem-solving with perspective. Two annual exhibitions and the December Art and Craft Sales also took place.

In 1989 Pam Shepherd became Secretary, Mary Seabrook was Chairman, Una Ridley was Treasurer and Norman Southorn was Programme Organiser. A stimulating programme continued, including regular visits by the versatile historian and artist Christine Shaw. By 1991 annual subscriptions had been raised to £4 and £2 for senior citizens.

In the autumn of 1997 the Programme Organisers were Pam Rawlins, Beverley Chamberlain and Prue King, Mary Seabrook continued as Chairman and Jessie Holt as Bookings Secretary. In 1998 Una Ridley died. She had been Treasurer for over twenty years and the legacy of her careful management benefits the Club today.

In the year 2000, weekly meetings are on Wednesday evenings in Manor Lodge. Annual subscriptions are £8 and £6 for senior citizens. There are two exhibitions, coinciding with the Carnival and the Abbots Langley Festival of the Arts, and a December art and craft sale. There is a monthly programme of speakers to which visitors are welcomed for a fee of £1. A portrait evening and a painting day at Redbournbury Watermill are planned.

Abbots Langley is fortunate to have an Art Club, and it would be good to see it continue as part of village life for many years to come.

A Day in my Life, November 1998

Audrey Ashby

The day started at 7 am when I got up, had breakfast with my husband and then he left for work. I washed up and left home in my car at 7.40. Ten minutes later I arrived at my daughter's house after picking up my newspaper en route. One of my grandchildren leaves for school with his father for the school run on his way to work, and I give the other two boys their breakfast and then hang out my daughter's washing in the garden – it is a fine day.

At 8.40 am I take the two boys to school, arriving for 9 am, and then return home to read my letters and the newspaper while enjoying a cup of coffee.

Today I have arranged to meet someone at Bedmond Village Hall, and I take photographs as the hall is about to be demolished. I spend an hour in the village – it is ideal for photography, the

The old Bedmond Village Hall, 1998. Photo: Ken Durtnall

autumn colours are superb. By 11.30 I can make my way home, arriving at 12.30 to have lunch and watch the TV news programme on ITV. I check my husband's greenhouse as frost is forecast, then pick the few remaining tomatoes and close the greenhouse down for the year.

At 3 pm I begin preparations for the evening meal, stopping for a cup of tea, and then sort my folder ready for the evening's committee meeting of the Abbots Langley Local History Society in the Abbots Langley library. At 5 pm I cook dinner, and after clearing it away and washing up I get ready to go out at 7 pm for the 7.30 meeting – which ends at 10.

I arrive home at 10.30 ready for a hot drink and a good night's rest.

Retiring early? Not in Abbots Langley – we might miss something!

Sue Avery

I don't know if many people retire to Abbots Langley. It's not on the south coast, has few retirement homes and no Bingo Hall. We retired here ten years ago by accident. A house was responsible. It came on the market at the right moment, and we couldn't resist it. The end of full-time work was on the horizon for both of us, so we moved three miles down the Bedmond Road and settled in a village we hardly knew. St Albans, Hemel Hempstead, and the bit in between, were familiar ground, but there was unfamiliar territory between Leverstock Green and Watford.

It proved to be a very fortuitous accident. Our lives have changed dramatically in ways which neither of us would have been able to imagine or foresee. I suppose, if we had been asked to look ahead, we would have predicted more leisure, time with the family, time for regular hobbies and interests, more reading, gardening, pottering and so on. Our three married children were producing babies and doubtless saw us as readily available baby-sitters. Actually, so did we for a short while!

Well, it's just not been like that. There's no aimless drifting in Abbots Langley for anyone who hasn't got a cast iron excuse like full employment. A great variety of local interest groups have infiltrated our new way of life, and our child caring services have to be booked well in advance. "What do you do, gallivanting round Abbots Langley in the evenings?" we have been asked.

Firstly there's entertainment. Abbots Langley has a Dramatic Society, a Choir, an Orchestra and a Light Operatic Society. They all perform at least twice a year, producing excellent amateur entertainment, and easily reached on foot. Then there are the restaurants. At present there are three high class Indian Restaurants, a Chinese Take-away, Fish and Chips and an Off-Licence. No drink-driving or parking worries to spoil eating out. We couldn't believe our luck!

That may sound enough, but there's more. Abbots Langley is not insular. There is imported entertainment as well. In the last six months alone, we have had a concert given by Neva-Russicum, a six-voiced Russian "a cappella" choir from St Petersburg. Their singing of Orthodox church music and Russian folk songs would have been special anywhere, but to hear them in St Lawrence church was an amazing privilege. Recently this was followed by an evening of 17th century transalpine music performed by a group called Ricordo, on period instruments. These included a Viola de Gamba and a Theorbo, unfamiliar to most of the audience. The latter is a four-foot high lute with a double peg board, and looks impossible to play. In the right hands it wasn't of course, and the sounds and improvisations were fascinating and suitably described as Stylus Phantasticus. Fantastic indeed for a village church concert. Next month (yes, there's more to come) we have a visit from the Chiltern Philharmonia Orchestra and Choir. Faure's Requiem and Beethoven's 8th Symphony are on the programme in

St Lawrence Church again, and we shall not miss that. I'm really sorry if this sounds like showing off, but it does all happen here and we are grateful for it.

Weekday evenings offer clubs and societies for shared interests. Local History, Bell Ringing, Flower Arranging, Horticulture, Bridge, Ex-service Men, Scouts, Guides, Youth, Over 50s, are just a few of the wide range of activities on offer. We have each taken our pick and joined in where interest led us. That takes over several more evenings. Plenty of sport is on offer, but we seem to have used up all surplus energy getting to and from all the other activities.

Lastly, but probably the group of activities that has changed our lives the most, are those which rely on volunteers. A busy Parish Council, a Citizens Advice Bureau, a fund-raising Hospice Shop, a flourishing Red Cross branch, a branch of Good Neighbours, all rely on unpaid workers. The same applies to the many supportive or fund-raising groups associated with the village churches or local branches of National Charities. Involvement with any of these is probably as beneficial to the giver as to the receiver. We hope that involvement with some of these has stimulated our diminishing brain cells into more activity than they were expecting. Learning curves have been steep, but pleasure in achievement has been very rewarding: new horizons, broader minds, increased knowledge, and enjoyable friendships. Anything that helps get our own lives in perspective is helpful. Society often seems unjust, but there is much to give us hope. Abbots Langley is full of people who are quietly trying to improve the quality of other people's lives, and we are very glad we are part of that community.

The word "retirement" cannot be used to describe our life here for the last ten years. We look forward to the next decade of being too busy to babysit.

A Day in my Life

Brian Hibberd

The day started fairly early for me. I find as I get older that the brain doesn't really cope with anything very serious by the time evening is getting close, so two or three times a week I make an earlyish start while the brain is reasonably active. Not too early, though, about 7 am.

It began with an hour or so on the thinking and method of Socrates. Tomorrow I shall be leading a study session as a tutor for the WEA – Workers' Education Association. It's a long time since it was really for "workers" and I have a typically middle-class group, all female and with an average age even older than mine. The course is on Religious Philosophy. Today I have to make sure that I not only know my stuff but also that I can present it in an interesting and varied way.

A break for breakfast: we rarely have a cooked breakfast now, and eat grapefruit, cereal, and toast with coffee or tea while the news team on Radio 4 keeps us informed about national and international developments.

Then, it's off to battle against the traffic on the M25. The battle begins well before that and it takes me over ten minutes to get onto the slip road less than a mile away. I sit and reflect on why I am doing this when I supposedly retired four years ago. Still, it's good to keep your hand in. The Head of the school I am going to is a friend who asked me to cover the gap left when her Religious Studies teacher left. My role is to teach the small examination groups. I have six girls in Year 10 who are studying the idea of religious festivals and calendars; four in Year 11 looking at beliefs as expressed in creeds, and two in the Sixth Form currently studying Luke's Gospel. It's a full teaching morning and takes a lot of preparation. I have to make sure that we are covering all the sections of their exam syllabus and that there is time to explain and illustrate things they find difficult or foreign to their usual way of thinking. There will be some homework to mark from today's teaching and some exams to set for the beginning of next term.

After a full morning's teaching I face a very different afternoon: two hours standing in the Watford Oxfam shop wearing a badge proclaiming me as "Security". It's an annual pre-Christmas task, and consists of trying to look sufficiently alert and sharp-eyed to deter would-be thieves. "Fancy having to have Security people at an Oxfam shop" I have heard several people say. I'm afraid if you're into thieving you don't usually think about who may lose out when you steal – you just make use of whatever opportunities come your way. "After all, you're a charity, aren't you?" was the indignant protest of somebody caught trying to get away with some donated goods!

Back home at about 4 pm and I can spend an hour or so with a cup of tea and a Terry Pratchett novel. My son got me reading him when he said that something I had written reminded him of the Pratchett humour. I have been a devoted fan ever since!

We enjoy "Neighbours" on TV, followed by the News, with food on trays balanced on our laps and prepared, I confess, by Pat whilst I was reading. Then it's my turn to do the washing up while The Archers is on the radio – Pat is the fan, not me!

Then it's off to the Barn to do "front of house" for the Abbots Langley Players. I usually act, but I'm not in this one. We've had a difficult year with problems about getting younger people to make the kind of commitment you need if you're going to act. Any amateur group tries to arrive at as polished and professional a production as possible. That takes a lot of rehearsing and time given over to learning the lines. The demands made by people's work and the need to be seen to be committed precludes real commitment to anything else. We had to cancel our Autumn production as a result of casting difficulties and settle for a smaller effort for an invited audience rather than a public one. A bit of a blow for the group. Tonight went well, though, lots of humour, some very strong language, and a good deal of pathos. I managed to persuade the audience to buy some raffle tickets and make a voluntary contribution to the funds as well as enjoying a good performance and a friendly chat over tea and coffee.

A longish day, and I'm beginning to feel my age. I can't help feeling quite satisfied, though.

Nature Notes

Sue and Dave Noise

For the past twenty-one years we have walked our dogs around the two fields between Standfield and Manor House Crescent, part of the old Manor House grounds. Over the years we have seen many lovely sights during balmy evenings when the Spotted Flycatchers were seen darting out from the hedges catching midges and flies. Then, as dusk advanced, bats would begin taking over with their erratic style of flying as they took a further toll of the insect population. The hedgerows used to look magnificent in their various seasonal moods. I have taken photographs of the trees and hedges on many occasions in the past, especially some of a comparatively rare hoar-frost and others of them in their beautiful autumnal colours or trees heavily snow laden in winter.

The bird population seems to vary annually. Three or four years ago it was very common to hear Owls hooting around these fields and sometimes, if we were lucky, they could be seen gliding silently across from one side of the field to the other as dusk settled. We occasionally saw a Green Woodpecker, too. Sadly, we haven't heard an Owl here for some time, but I am pleased to say that earlier this year (1999) we did see four Green Woodpeckers together – two adults and two fledglings – the latter being taught to feed themselves. Certainly a pleasant sight.

However, what saddens us most of all is the gradual decline in the general condition of the undergrowth, which is so often

The old oak tree on the cricket ground (Manor House field) with its replacement already planted. Photo: February 2000, Reg Nice

trampled down and broken, the damaged trees, their branches hanging dead, discarded litter, bottles and tins, etc., and the systematic reduction in the bluebell population over the last few years.

Perhaps, then, it is time for us all to become more aware of our surroundings by encouraging sufficiently, the protection and development of our local heritage, where nature and the environment are concerned? How sad it would be if we could no longer enjoy these delights of nature. Let's hope that with the start of a new millennium we can begin to generate a new appreciation of our surroundings and so help to protect the many habitats of wildlife for the future.

Birds seen in our garden (Standfield, Abbots Langley, 1999): House Sparrow, Hedge Sparrow, Brambling, Starling, Song Thrush, Redwing, Chaffinch, Goldfinch, Blackcap, Pied Wagtail, Collared Dove, Magpie, Blue Tit, Coal Tit, Sparrow Hawk, Green Woodpecker, Tree Sparrow, Dunnock, Wren, Robin, Blackbird,

Mistle Thrush, Fieldfare, Greenfinch, Bullfinch, Willow Warbler, Crow, Wood Pigeon, Jay, Long Tailed Tit, Great Tit, Heron.

Birds seen from the garden: Black Headed Gull, Swallow, Swift.

A Day in my Life

Peter Tomson

Born in 1926, I retired in 1990 after more than thirty years as General Practitioner in Abbots Langley and since then I have been able fully to enjoy the Abbot's House garden. The garden occupies most of my days, it is now my "raison d'être", and my wife Susan and I love creating and maintaining it.

A typical day begins with the alarm at 7.15 am, and on December 10 1999 I was, unusually, up first. A cool day – decided on vest, shirt, two sweaters, trousers, tidyish. By 7.30 we were breakfasting on bran flakes, Sue's own homemade brown milk bread with no butter or marmalade, and "real" coffee, and I read the News section of the Independent. Then at 8 o'clock I drove in the Citröen ZX to Chipperfield to collect cases of wine from a friend, mainly to use for Open Days and Concerts in the Barn. Back home again to find the post had been delivered, and opened a few Christmas cards, and then off for an appointment with the local optician. He noted "little change, but can make reading easier". Sue and I erected a small bookcase for the spare room and reorganised the furniture, and then I changed into jeans and an old shirt and sweaters and gum boots ready for a session in the garden, but had a cup of Maxwell House instant coffee first; we have decided that Nescafé is immoral because of their policy of selling baby milk in third world countries.

At last I go into the garden and open the greenhouse and tunnel, inspect seedlings and decide against watering. I filled in a bit more of the old compost pit with old rubble to make an alpine bed – this was hard work! Then looked at the proposed

Peter and Susan Tomson, Abbot's House Gardens, 1998. Photo: Eve Durtnall

enlargement of the mahonia bed and decided that David Baxter might help to remove the exposed old concrete slab. I wonder for what it had been the base? I moved a rooted clematis to the wall ready for a hole to be dug for it, and tidied up leaves and weeds, and cut back overhanging plants, for composting or the leaf-mould pit.

At this point Elizabeth Manning found me in the garden and asked me to write a diary of a typical day in my life to include in the Abbots Langley Local History Society archive for posterity, and then Pat and Ray Holmes called to deliver a Christmas card and ask my thoughts about using ascorbic acid to help root geranium cuttings – but I have no knowledge about this. Sue then went off to work as a volunteer at the Oxfam shop, and I continued working in the garden until about 1 o'clock. I lunched on bread and sardines, salami and cheese, a Cox's apple from the garden and two bananas, and some more Maxwell House instant coffee, and read the Review section of the Independent.

Back into the garden for more leaf raking and general tidying, and by 3.45 I closed the tunnel and greenhouse, brought in the washing, and changed back into tidier clothes ready to go to the Red Cross Blithe Spirits Christmas party. I arrived in time for carols, and enjoyed seeing old friends and ex-patients.

By 5 o'clock I was back home with another coffee reading the Watford Observer, disappointed there was nothing of particular interest to me. After emptying the washing-up machine I lit the wood fire in the panelled room upstairs and began work on this diary on the computer. Sue came home and I helped her put away the shopping – she has caught my cold and is streaming. Took a few minutes to help Sue in the kitchen and because it's Friday we indulge in a gin and french (dry Vermouth). Time to check the e-mail and there's one from British Telecom trying to persuade us to shop by e-mail (NO) and one from son David suggesting amendments to my review of a book for his mini-journal. Receive visit from eight-year old daughter of tenant with rest of the rent for the cottage, and then a visit from a neighbour with wine to store in our cellar. Back to the computer for some more of this diary, and then down to the kitchen to help Sue with supper which we ate in the panelled room in front of the wood fire, watching the "Task Force" gardening programme on TV. Supper consisted of cod and a sauce, mashed potatoes (from our garden), and frozen peas, followed by our raspberries and currants from the freezer, and crème fraîche, with South African Chardonnay.

Back to the computer again to print off labels for our Christmas card envelopes, and some more typing, and at around 11 pm it was time for bath and bed. Read in bed for a while, "The River at the Centre of the World" by Simon Winchester – a historical travelogue about the Yangtze.

As on most days, the garden occupies most of my time. It is just under two acres, and is a garden of rooms, sunken, formal and Mediterranean gardens, mixed borders, unusual shrubs and trees, annual and wildflower meadows, and this winter's creation which is a raised alpine and ericaceous bed. I am vain – I like showing it to other people, we love sharing it and it gives a lot of pleasure to others, and we open the garden for charity about five times a year in the National Open Gardens scheme as well as for local events.

On being Retired in Abbots Langley as the Millennium Approaches

John Sutton

A company pension, following redundancy at fifty, allowed me not to have to work until sixty-five when the National Retirement Pension became payable (five years earlier for women despite their having a statistical longer life).

Retirement at that age obviously offers different openings compared with a man retiring twelve years later, but today's pensioner of sixty-five is generally still an active person.

But whatever your age, Abbots Langley is a splendid place to live in retirement. Firstly, compared with places where people go to retire, it is not full of elderly people. This gives more opportunity to mix with younger people which as well as benefiting one mentally, enables societies to flourish which rely on young people for support.

Currently it has its own Post Office, two banks, and a variety of shops. There are many parts of the country where this isn't the case, and an expensive bus journey is necessary to shop and obtain one's pension.

The essential health services are all present, with a group practice of about six doctors occupying the recently extended Vine House. Here can also be found nurses to treat non-serious ailments and run health checks. For more serious events, the local hospital is only five miles away. We are also fortunate in having a dentist, an optician, a chiropodist and an osteopath practising in

High Street from the site of Causeway House, February 2000. Photo: Reg Nice

the village. Two dispensing chemists complete the picture. That does not include services provided by the hospital in Watford, and care services provided by Hertfordshire County Council et al.

Where many town high streets have found that the traditional shops have been replaced by banks and building societies, Abbots Langley has become beset with restaurants. In the high street of approximately thirty premises, we have four Indian, two Chinese, a fish and chip shop, a café and two of the three pubs having meals available. One doesn't need to eat at home!

Most days of the week the local library is open. This was built on the site of the old village schools. As well as books for borrowing, both fiction and non-fiction, there is a very good reference section, and also video cassettes, tape cassettes, compact discs are available for hire, and "talking books" for the blind.

The village is also very fortunate in having a large number of local societies catering for both cultural and sporting enthusiasts.

Abbots Langley Library, High Street, February 2000. Photo: Reg Nice

The local Gilbert & Sullivan Society is probably the most well known, since it performs shows at the Palace Theatre in Watford, and has also been invited to take part in the 1999 International Festival at Buxton. Actors as well as singers are catered for. Whilst the person of retirement age is unlikely to take part in the village football or cricket teams, the tennis courts witness players of this age. A more likely venue is the bowling club, and the green behind the Scouts Headquarters in Langley Road is very busy during the summer months.

Allotments are kept by both young and old, but it is the retired person who can generally make their second home in one of the sheds to be found on any of the sites owned by the Parish Council. Often the allotment holder will be a member of the Horticultural Society where seeds, fertilisers, etc. may be obtained at a very good discount.

The ladies have their own Societies such as the Mothers' Union and Women's Fellowship which are attached to St Lawrence

Church; the Women's Institute; The National Women's Register, etc. All these societies are listed in the library, and most of them in the Parish Directory within the church magazine "Outlook".

For the older person there are a number of clubs – the Evergreens (for the over-sixties); Derby & Joan Clubs; and Day Centres for those who don't normally get out. This last is staffed by volunteers, including car owners who collect and return those who require transport. Meals on wheels are delivered to the housebound, and retirement and nursing homes exist for those who are unable to lead an independent existence. Volunteers drive the Good Neighbours minibus, taking those unable to travel by bus to the local shops and further afield. I am pleased to say that to date I am not in need of any of these services, and admit to some feelings of guilt as neither have I volunteered to help with them.

If I want some exercise, the countryside is close at hand. The Parish Council have published a number of walks around the village following the many footpaths that exist, both through the village and across the fields. The "Busy Bees" – an organisation for the over-fifties run by Watford Borough Council – also organises rambles once a month, covering the surrounding area.

If gardening and decorating begin to pall, or the weather is inclement, then one need not feel so guilty about tuning into the radio or television, where a huge variety of entertainment abounds twenty-four hours a day.

A Weekend in November 1999

Roger Yapp

I have chosen to write about the first weekend in November 1999. It was a fairly hectic weekend for the Yapp family in Abbots Langley...

Friday 5th November

"Remember, remember, the 5th of November, Gunpowder, Treason and Plot". I think that that is how the old poem goes. Friday 5th November was not a fairly routine day at work. I am currently employed as the Computer Network Services Manager by the Canada Life Assurance Company and work at their offices in Potters Bar. The organisation's Head Office is in Toronto, Canada, and throughout 1998 and 1999 the company had been working towards "demutualising" – which in common terms means that instead of being "owned" by its policy-holders, the company is floated on the Stock Market (the Toronto Market in this case) and "ownership" moves to shareholders. Friday 5th November was the date that Canada Life chose to demutualise, and to celebrate this we were allowed to attend work in smart, casual clothes instead of the traditional suits that are our normal office garb. We were also treated to an indoor barbecue lunch, which was excellent, with a free beer and loads of food. The afternoon was however fairly routine, with a couple of meetings, before leaving for home to prepare for attending our neighbours' annual Fireworks Party.

I arrived home at around 6.30 pm, probably about half an hour earlier than normal. My wife, Jonquil, had bought a box of fireworks, and some beer and wine, and we put on some old clothes and outdoor shoes before we went next door for the party. We checked that our three cats – Mrs Miggins (named after the character in the Black Adder TV series), Bob and Jake, were safely indoors, and away from the bangs and flashes of the fireworks party. We left Buster Bunny (our rabbit) in his cage on the patio. He is nine now, and is the veteran of several Bonfire Nights, and seems to be fine snuggled up in the hay and straw in his hutch.

Our neighbours, John and Irene Field, have organised a fireworks party for their four sons – Daniel, Matthew, Tom and Jack – for as long as they can remember, and each year the same group of friends and family are invited. Over the years the number of people attending the party has grown, and nowadays about 50 people are crammed into their garden. This year the fireworks were even better than before, and Irene worked tirelessly to provide hot soup, hotdogs and burgers for everyone – she even catered for the vegetarians in the group with veggie-burgers. Unfortunately as the display unfolded it started to rain, but undaunted we continued and I'm sure our fireworks were the best around. We left the party at about 11.30 pm, wet and muddy and our clothes smelling heavily of smoke from the bonfire that John had built. John and his partner (Roy Barnes) run a local building firm (BarnesField) and they are always able to get sufficient wood to make an excellent bonfire each year.

Saturday 6th November

Every Saturday morning I take my 89-year old mother to Sainsbury's SavaCentre at London Colney, so that she has the opportunity to select her own shopping for the week ahead. My mother (Olive) is 90 on 16 November and has reached a good old age, but in 1992 she had a fall in Clacton and broke her hip. Since then she has been disabled and although she can walk, she is finding this more and more difficult, and at the SavaCentre we can book the use of a free wheelchair and specially designed trolley which makes shopping fairly easy.   We always arrive around 10.45 and leave somewhere around 12.30 and if we have time we have a cup of tea and a chat in the hypermarket's restaurant.

I spent the afternoon watching the Final of the Rugby World Cup between Australia (the new favourites) and France (who the previous week had surprisingly come from behind to beat the tournament favourites, New Zealand). The Final was held at the new Millennium Stadium in Cardiff, which has replaced the old Cardiff Arms Park. The weather for the Final was not good (rain), and there was a lot of discussion prior to the game as to whether or not the organisers should close the retractable roof (and keep the elements out) or leave it open and let the players play in their normal weather conditions. In the end they chose to leave the roof open for the game, but keep it closed until just before kick-off. The game was fairly uneventful, as the Australians were just too good and organised, and the French looked jaded after their previous week's win. Australia ran out winners. As a nation they have won so much this year in the world of sport.

In the evening Jonquil sang in a concert at a church in Harrow. She is a member of the Harrow Choral Society and the choir sings a lot of classical church-type music – Masses and Glorias and that sort of thing. I didn't go along this time as I had already seen and heard the concert, and this was a repeat performance at quite a small church (hence it was sold out) and was organised as a fundraising exercise for church funds. Jonquil joined the choir about four years ago and really enjoys the singing – so much so that she is honing her skills by having additional singing and piano lessons (the latter to help her sightread music).

Sunday 7th November

On Sunday morning I set about laying some cork tiles on the bathroom floor. Over the previous weeks Jonquil had painstakingly, and almost single-handedly, redecorated the bathroom, and all that was left was to replace the floor. After cutting some plywood to size and nailing it down to the wooden floorboards (to make a nice flat surface) I progressed to laying the cork tiles that we had bought from Sainsbury's Homebase in St Albans Road, Watford. Once I had measured everything, and planned how best to lay the tiles, it was a very complicated task to cut out all of the angles, and I managed to get floor adhesive everywhere – at 6'7" I am just too big to fit into our small bathroom, and wherever I put the opened container of glue I always seemed to get adhesive on my back, elbows or legs. It was destined to take me the best part of eight hours to finally finish the job.

Whilst I was upstairs in the bathroom, Jonquil remained in the kitchen, tidying up, starting to prepare the vegetables for our evening meal, and listening to "The Archers Omnibus" on Radio 4. This is a weekly ritual – catching up on the stories of the farming people of Ambridge. Midway through the morning our nineteen-year old daughter Francine telephoned from Israel to say that she was returning home later in the day. Francine is adopted and has lived with us since the age of two. Her sister Teresa (30 this year) has just completed a degree course at London University and has always been in contact and is very much part of our family. Whilst studying she has continued to work at the Middlesex Hospital in London, where she is a qualified nurse.

After completing her GCSEs (General Certificate of Secondary Education) at Kings Langley School, Francine attended Watford College and passed a BTEC qualification in Performing Arts which will enable her to continue and study at University. She completed her course at Watford College in June 1998, and set off travelling in July, firstly visiting Kos (where she worked waitressing and in bars for several months) before moving on through Rhodes, Cyprus and eventually settling in Israel. She had returned home in May 1999 to be the surprise guest at my 50th birthday, but returned to Israel in July. Her decision to return to England at this point in November was quite a shock for us, as whilst decorating the bathroom we had used Francine's bedroom as a "dumping ground" for the paints, etc., etc., etc. We really didn't expect her for another week or so, in time for my mother's 90th birthday on 16th November, and Teresa's graduation at the Barbican in London later in the month. Suddenly she was returning, the bathroom floor needed finishing and Francine's bedroom needed cleaning and clearing up.

It was 12 noon and she would arrive at 10.00 pm that night. *Another normal weekend for Yapp household in Abbots Langley.*

For the record we made it. Francine arrived a little late and was met at Gatwick by her sister. She travelled back with Teresa and stayed overnight at her room in the Nurses' Home in London.

David Miller – Milkman

The day starts at 2 am for me, when I get up, have a light breakfast and travel by car to the Express Dairy Distribution depot at North Watford, arriving just after 2.30 am. I am self-

David Miller, Milkroundsman, 2000. Photo: Elizabeth Manning

employed, acting as a franchisee for Express Dairy. I pay for the hire of the milk float, management fees, insurance and for milk and produce from the monies collected. I have to dress suitably to encounter all types of weather. The company provides a basic uniform as well as waterproof wear. On a bad day the rain can blow right through the vehicle in one door and out the other; fortunately there are not too many like this!

The "milk float" is a purpose-built vehicle propelled by two huge batteries, being electrically charged overnight. It carries 25 crates on a single layer, each crate holds 20 pints of milk. There is a box at the back for carrying provisions, and a small compartment for perishable goods which are kept cool by an ice plate refrozen daily.

I load the day's milk for delivery onto my milk float, that is, about 500 pints *(one pint equals roughly half a litre)* of whole milk, semi-skimmed, skimmed, homogenised, and the odd Gold Top – full cream Channel Island milk. About 70% of this milk is low fat. I also carry a variety of other products: bread, cheese, eggs, potatoes, cakes, fruit juice, bacon, butter, and on occasions other promotional products. These additional groceries are handy for customers who find they have run out of them.

At about 3 am I leave the depot travelling three miles to Abbots Langley to deliver milk to about 500 doorsteps, starting in Follett Drive. My route comprises Follett Drive, Trowley Rise, Oak Green, Greenways, Popes Road, Breakspear Road, Garden Road, Marlin Square, Adrian Road, High Street, The Crescent, Hanover Gardens, Langley Road, part of Abbots Road, Standfield, Dell Meadow, Parsonage Close, ending with a delivery of children's one-third pint cartons to Abbots Langley School. The delivery route always includes a stop for more breakfast! Written notes are my main means of communication at this early hour, not a foolproof system as sometimes the notes are not seen on dark mornings. I return to the milk depot between 10 am and 2 pm depending on the day, trying to be finished early on a Saturday. I return home and have lunch, and go to bed for two or three hours. I usually spend the remaining daylight hours in the allotment as this is my main interest.

After dinner I spend an average one hour per day completing and updating my rounds' books, which list all customers and their daily requirements. These books, I understand, are soon to be replaced by hand-held computers.

Towards the end of the week I then retrace part of the route, collecting payment from customers. Also included is a basket delivery of cakes and provisions for many elderly customers in Oak Green which is time-consuming but greatly appreciated by many who are unable to get to the village shops. Conversations on the round tend to be short due to the large number of customers. I enjoy meeting my customers and the open-air life of being a milkman.

The day finishes at about 10 pm, going to bed in preparation for the next day/night – day and night are often confused when getting up ...

Nicholas Breakspear Week in Abbots Langley 24 September to 1 October 2000

Alan S Johnson

Nicholas Breakspear Week in September 2000 gave Abbots Langley the opportunity to celebrate the ninth centenary of the birth of this great man of Europe, who was the only Englishman to become Pope.

Nicholas was born in 1100 at Bedmond Farm in the parish of Abbots Langley, Hertfordshire. Presumably after the death of Nicholas' mother, his father Robert Breakspear became a monk of St Albans Abbey. When Nicholas was about 18 years old, he too applied to enter St Albans Abbey but he was refused admission on the grounds that he had had too little schooling to qualify for entrance.

Undeterred by this refusal, Nicholas went abroad to study, briefly to St Denys in Paris and then to other places. He finally came to Avignon and it was here in 1130 that he became a monk in the Augustinian Abbey of St Rufus. He was elected Abbot in 1137 and came to the notice of the then Pope, Eugenius III, who recognised his qualities and made him Bishop and Cardinal and sent him on a mission to war-torn Scandinavia. Nicholas restored peace and order to the local churches and monasteries, and set up two new archbishoprics. After four years, by then widely recognised as a man of integrity and strength, he returned to Rome to find that Engenius III had died and his successor was Anastasius IV. Anastasius was a quiet, peaceful old man of ninety and within a year Anastasius too was dead, and in November 1154 Nicholas found himself unanimously elected Pope. He took the name Adrian IV.

During the summer of 2000 in Abbots Langley village library and in other places a pictorial display of the main events of

Catholic Church, The Crescent, February 2000. Photo: Reg Nice

Nicholas Breakspear's life and travels was mounted, and for this week of celebration in September there was a banner across the High Street and as well as floral displays around the road signs in Breakspear Road, Popes Road and Adrian Road.

On Sunday morning 24 September in both St Saviour's and St Lawrence churches a short introduction to the life of Nicholas Breakspear was read. The two churches, Roman Catholic and Anglican respectively, co-operated closely in remembering this man, recognising that his life was set in times long before the Reformation divided Protestant from Roman Catholic.

On Sunday afternoon, 24 September, an historical walk beginning at St Lawrence Church visited the plaque by the roadside in Bedmond near the site where Nicholas was born, and progressed to the floral displays in the village ending in St Saviour's Church by the bust of Nicholas Breakspear as Pope Adrian IV. Each day throughout the week further instalments of The Life of Nicholas Breakspear were read after 10 am Mass at St Saviour's.

On Thursday evening 28 September in St Lawrence Church, the Abbots Langley Local History Society presented a lecture by the

Reverend Canon Anders Bergquist entitled "From Bedmond to Trondheim to Rome: the career of Nicholas Breakspear".

On Sunday 1st October at St Saviour's, Solemn Mass was celebrated in memory of the life and papacy of Nicholas Breakspear, Pope Adrian IV, followed later in the day by two of the daily monastic services with which Nicholas would have been familiar as monk and Abbot: Vespers of Sunday at 4 pm in St Saviour's, and Sung Compline in St Lawrence Church at 8 pm. This brought to a close the week of commemoration at the site where Robert Breakspear and his wife first brought their new son to church and named him Nicholas, in 1100.

This man had been born and brought up as Nicholas Breakspear among the farms and cottages of twelfth century Abbots Langley, had had dealings with the emperor Frederic Barbarossa and the English King Henry II, and died on 1st September 1159 as Pope Adrian IV.

Colourful flowers, provided by the Abbots Langley & District Horticultural Society, adorn road signs in Abbots Langley during Nicholas Breakspear Week 2000. Photo: Mike Quinton